The Monday Morning Guide to Comprehension

LEE GUNDERSON

Pippin Publishing Limited

The first excerpt on p. 9 is from *Our Big Book* by W.S. Gray.
Copyright © 1951 by W.S. Gray. Reprinted by permission
of Scott, Foresman and Company.
The second excerpt on p. 9 is from *Miami Linguistic Reading*
by R.F. Robinett, P.E. Bell & P.M. Rojas. Copyright © 1971
by R.F. Robinett, P.E. Bell & P.M. Rojas. Reprinted
by permission of D.C. Heath and Co.
The excerpt on p. 12 is from "An Experimental Study
of the Eye-Voice Span in Reading" by G.T. Buswell
(*Supplementary Educational Monographs*, #20). Reprinted
by permission of the University of Chicago Press.
The excerpt on p. 22 is from *The Judge* by Harve Zemach.
Copyright © 1969 by Harve Zemach. Reprinted by permission
of Farrar, Straus and Giroux, Inc.

Edited by Dyanne Rivers
Designed by John Zehethofer
Printed and bound by Kromar Printing Ltd.

Canadian Cataloguing in Publication Data

Gunderson, Lee
    The Monday morning guide to comprehension

(The Pippin teacher's library ; 13)
Includes bibliographical references.
ISBN 0-88751-052-3
1. Reading (Elementary) — Language experience approach. 2. Reading comprehension. I. Title. II. Series.

LB1573.7.G86 1993   372.4'1   C93-093935-2

ISBN 0-88751-052-3

10   9   8   7   6   5   4   3   2   1

To Olga Charlotte Griffin

The author gratefully acknowledges the assistance of Patricia Whitney, who researched and prepared the bibliographies of children's books.

CONTENTS

60,000 Worksheets…and Counting 7

A Little Sunday Night Theory 8
What Is Reading? 8
Language As an Interactive Process 10
Emergent Literacy 13
Theory in the Classroom 15
Summary 15

How Many Webs Did Charlotte Spin? 16

Reading—An Interactive Process 16
The Directed Reading-Thinking Activity 17
Literary Appreciation 25
Summary 26

Why, What, When, How? 27

Comprehension Levels 27
Literal-Level Comprehension Strategies 28
Inferential-Level Comprehension Strategies 31
Critical and Evaluative-Level Comprehension 37
Summary 43

The Square of the Hypotenuse Equals… 44

Why Is Content Reading So Hard? 44
Do I Really Want to Know That…? 46
What Everyone Should Know 47
What Students Should Know 52
What Do We Already Know? 53
Summary 61

The Best Widgets in the World *63*

Purpose of Reading and Reading Rate *63*
But Can They Read It Independently? *72*
SQ3R *76*
Content Webs *78*
Finding Out If Students Have Content Reading Problems *79*
Summary *82*

Keeping the Warehouse in Order *83*

Thirty Students in a Single Room *86*
The 10 Per Cent Solution *87*
The 20 Per Cent Solution *91*
Basketball Is a Nice Game! *92*
Who's on First? *99*
Going Whole Hog *103*
Summary *109*

Is an "A" by Any Other Name as Sweet? *110*

What Grade Did I Get? *110*
What's Her Level? *111*
Authentic Assessment *112*
What Parents Really Ought to Know *118*
And Tomorrow Is Monday *119*

Bibliography *121*

Wordless Picture Books *121*
Predictable Books *123*
Professional References *126*

60,000 WORKSHEETS...

AND COUNTING

It was eight o'clock on a Sunday evening. I faced the prospect of spending the final hours of an otherwise wonderful weekend correcting students' reading and math workbooks. The first wasn't so bad. It was Paul Taylor's and he seldom filled in the wrong word or circled the wrong letter. Nevertheless, I resented the intrusion into my weekend and began to bemoan the lot of teachers.

I flipped the pages of several workbooks, admiring the care with which I had red-marked incorrect responses and neatly recorded grades at the top of each page. Paul's workbook was filled with marks that revealed his expertise. One of the stories he'd read was about the Greek gods, their epic deeds and the mortals' reactions to them. In his workbook, Paul had filled in all the right answers—but had he really comprehended the story? Had he enjoyed it? Had it inspired him to think about the Greek influence in our lives?

My resentment at correcting the piles of worksheets was suddenly overtaken by a sense of guilt, a sense that I had committed the children to a prison-like sentence that required them to be punished after reading every story by answering worksheet questions. In this situation, why would they ever *want* to read anything? It seemed that the cumulative effect of my instruction was a pile of workbooks, hours of tedium for the eight- and nine-year-olds in my class, and behemothian efforts on my part to monitor each workbook like an auditor examining suspect bank records—all to do little more than create massive disinterest in reading among the students.

I stood up, gathered together the workbooks, and threw them into the garbage. It wasn't until later, as I was falling asleep, that I began to wonder, What am I going to do tomorrow? What am I going to do on Monday morning?

A Little Sunday Night Theory

Many teachers believe that research and theory are for ivory tower professors, individuals who may never have seen a real classroom with sweaty kids and occasional bloody noses, and that they, the classroom toilers, do what's right for students. This notion ignores the idea that all teaching is based on an internal model the teacher believes in, a model often adopted without thought, conviction or considered analysis. Many teachers seem to do what they remember *their* teachers doing, regardless of the consequences, much like assembly-line robots who piece together an automobile without ever knowing what the final product looks like, let alone its functions or purposes. They react because they've been programmed to react. Having students mindlessly fill in workbook blanks is based on faith and folklore, a kind of programming.

As Mary Ashworth notes, "There's nothing more practical than a good theory." Theory helps us examine our teaching in logical ways. Practically, it allows us to extend, expand and adapt all the activities that will be encountered in this book in logical and useful ways. It also gives us a reason for teaching, a real purpose.

What follows is a little theorizing, based on twenty-five years' experience in classrooms in North America and the Far East. It's short and sweet, but if you're anxious to get to the "cookbook" part of this text, I suggest you skip to the next chapter. Return to this section when you've read the rest of the book. It might even make more sense then.

What Is Reading?

Humans have read for about the last 5,000 years. Yet, ironically, there is still very little agreement about what reading is. Much of the confusion has to do with how wonderfully adaptive human beings are and how wonderfully creative researchers are in designing studies they think address reading.

In 1947, James McKeen Cattell published a work describing how his grandfather had, in 1889, used an ingenious machine to show briefly letters and words to subjects in psychological studies. In doing so, the elder Cattell may have originated the tradition of studying "reading" by looking at what happens when people try to recognize letters and words after seeing only flashes of them. His findings suggested that we learn words better and they remain in memory longer the more often we see them. This sounds a little like saying that we need practice to remember words, doesn't it?

The problem with studies that focus on words is that they require subjects to alter their normal reading behavior. These studies led researchers to develop a theory that broke down reading into parts—letters and words. Sometimes this is called the sub-skills- or skills-based reading model and it's the model many teachers implicitly believe in. It suggests that reading involves a large number of separate skills that learners must master in sequence—skills required to get ready to read (called, of course, readiness skills), skills related to letter-sound relationships (phonics), word recognition skills and, finally, comprehension skills.

For years, teachers taught these skills by printing high-frequency words on flash cards and requiring children to practice recognizing them until they could do so by sight. Consider the following classic text published in 1951:

Look, Jane.
Look, look.
See Dick.
See, see.
Oh, see.
See Dick.
Oh, see Dick.

Authors of textbooks designed for English as a second language students also adopted this "scientific" approach. The following is an example from a textbook for beginning ESL students:

Biff and Tiff
Biff
Tiff

Tiff.
Tiff!
Sit, Tiff.
Sit, Tiff, sit!
Biff is sitting.

In both cases, the vocabulary control is obvious. In the second case, the authors selected high-frequency vocabulary with regular spelling patterns (e.g., bit, fit, hit, sit). These texts were referred to as "linguistic" readers because they contained words with regular spelling patterns.

Publishers came to the aid of teachers by producing basal readers that carefully controlled vocabulary in several ways:

— Only high-frequency words were used in initial instruction.
— Only a few words were introduced at a time.
— Words were repeated often so that students would memorize them efficiently.
— Words were introduced and practiced in isolation (i.e., teachers became flashers).
— A standardized lesson plan involving the directed reading approach—DRA—was designed.

This model suggests that children come to comprehend a text by first associating sounds with letters, then putting together the sounds to produce words, then putting the words together to form sentences, and, finally, comprehending the sentences and, therefore, the overall message. It also suggests that there is a developmental sequence to mastering a hierarchy of skills both between and within language modes; that is, students learn first to speak and listen, then to read, and, finally, to write.

Language As an Interactive Process

In 1965, Ken Goodman proposed that reading is a psycholinguistic process in which readers act in a "top-down" fashion. They come to a text with expectations based on their knowledge of English syntax and semantics and their experience with the world. In his contribution to *Theoretical Models and Processes of Reading*, he suggested that a reader selects "the fewest, most productive cues necessary to produce guesses which are right the first time." In his view, miscues (instances in which what is read differs from what is on the page) are not always indications of poor reading. When a miscue doesn't alter the meaning of a sentence, it shows that the reader is comprehending. Indeed, miscues show that readers are actively predicting based on their understanding of the printed text. Predictions are based on a reader's knowledge of syntax (the systematic ordering of words in English), semantics (the meaning of words) and their own previous knowledge.

The idiomatic expressions we use so often in spoken English reveal the underlying processes involved in reading. For example, try filling in the blank in the following sentence:

As my mother says, you shouldn't cry over spilt _____.

This idiom illustrates the factors that interact predictably in English. I suspect that older native English speakers would unanimously identify the missing word. How do we know? Our knowledge of syntax tells us that the word can't be a verb or adjective—we wouldn't expect spilt "were" or spilt "heavy." A noun is appropriate, but not just any noun. We know from the structure of the sentence that the noun must be something like "houses" or "water" because there is no article before the adjective. If there were an indefinite article (i.e., "a"), then we would predict a singular noun like house. Because there isn't one, we predict a collective noun, such as "water," or a plural countable noun, such as "twigs." In fact, very good English as a second language speakers use this same knowledge to make predictions like these when they read unfamiliar idioms. A Chinese woman, for instance, used this kind of knowledge to suggest "woman" as the missing word in the idiom, "S/he is a blithering _____."

To their knowledge of syntax and semantics, native English speakers add a different kind of knowledge having to do with their cultural background. There is a direct relationship between age and knowledge of idioms. Tiong Lauw, a graduate student at the University of British Columbia, found that older native English speakers had a much wider repertoire of idioms than younger individuals. He conjectured that reading helps us acquire a greater knowledge of idiomatic terms then simply speaking a language. As we read, many different kinds of knowledge interact to help us predict words, sentences, concepts and outcomes. Consider the following invented idiom:

> There's nothing more radical in dealing with burned buffalo wings than turning to your mother and asking for her _____.

What word did you predict? Why? Analyze the different sources of knowledge you used to make your prediction.

Comprehension is creative and predictive. As we read, we make predictions based on many different kinds of knowledge. The following paragraph by Guy Buswell reveals that reading is more than simply decoding. Read it aloud quickly, without rehearsing.

> The boys' arrows were nearly gone so they sat down on the grass and stopped hunting. Over at the edge of the woods they saw Henry making a bow to a little girl who was coming down the road. She had tears in her dress and also tears in her eyes. She gave Henry a note which he brought over to the group of young hunters. Read to the boys, it caused great excitement. After a minute but rapid examination of their weapons, they ran down the valley. Does were standing at the edge of the lake making an excellent target.

The typical reader begins by miscuing on the word "bow," giving it the pronunciation associated with "bow and arrow" because the words "arrows" and "hunting" establish a kind of script that guides comprehension. Within the established "hunting" script, the word "bow" is decoded in a particular way. In this respect, the passage is misleading. The typical reader also produces the miscue "tears," as in "tears in her eyes," when reading "she had tears in her dress." This results from applying syntactic information while reading. In this position, the word would normally refer to crying because we would likely say "her dress was torn." "After a minute" is decoded to refer to time for the same kind of syntactic reasons.

This interactive view suggests that reading is a creative process, relying as much on personal cognitive information as on textual information. Holistic teachers view reading this way. The question of how we acquire the necessary interactive knowledge is another matter. In this case, whole language teachers look to research in emergent literacy.

Emergent Literacy

Some children are very fortunate. They come to school already knowing a great deal about reading and writing, apparently without direct instruction. During the 1970s and '80s, there was great interest in children who learned to read before they entered school. Many researchers observed the development of individual children growing up in environments where literacy and literacy activities were highly valued.

One of the first things noticed about these children is that they begin to scribble quite early and, when asked, report that they are writing. Quickly, they begin to make letters and letter-like forms. In fact, there appears to be a developmental sequence in which children begin to understand that print represents language. Studies by researchers such as Diane DeFord, Anne Dyson, Emilia Ferreiro, Marjorie Hipple and Elizabeth Sulzby indicate that the writing of preschoolers progresses through a series of developmental stages—scribbling (with meaning), perceiving print and drawing as synonymous, representing things with individual letters, writing initial consonants to represent words beginning with particular sounds, placing spaces between words, representing sounds with letters, inventing spellings, and producing the mature conventions of spelling and writing. Young children also learn to "read" environmental print—to recognize and understand the significance of visual stimuli like McDonalds' golden arches. They can produce and read their own material even though it bears little resemblance to the mature writing model produced by literate adults.

The traditional developmental sequence upon which many language programs are built—listening, speaking, reading, writing—is likely incorrect. For years, teachers who use these programs have mistakenly accepted that children should be involved in activities that help them learn speaking and listening skills, which should precede reading instruction, which itself should precede writing instruction.

Yet studies of emergent literacy find that youngsters who learn to read early don't acquire this skill separately, but rather as an activity well-integrated into other activities. These studies form the basis of an instructional model, not a language model, within which the interactive model of language is placed.

High-literacy homes, filled with literacy events and activities, copious written materials and individuals interested in reading and writing are the best language-learning environments yet created by human beings. Mothers and fathers are seen as readers, speakers, listeners and writers. They interact with their children, modeling the activities the children are learning. They use materials, such as children's books, that are interesting and meaningful to their youngsters.

Holistic teachers try to emulate in their classrooms these wonderful literacy-learning environments. Children are involved in interactive language activities. They read and write from the first day at school. Teachers use meaningful, interesting materials and focus on whole stories rather than parts.

Writing is always for a purpose and the teacher, believing that the process is more important than the product, doesn't correct it in the traditional way. A grandmother doesn't return a loving note with the grammar and spelling errors highlighted. She reacts to the message, not the form. Children select their own reading material because it interests them and this becomes part of their reading program. Subjects such as science and social studies are integrated into reading and language arts. At home, for instance, learning to read isn't separated from learning about dinosaurs.

The love of reading and writing is considered as important as the mechanics. Indeed, a teacher's goal is not to perfect the mechanics of the children's writing and reading, but rather to involve them actively in the process. Focusing on mechanics involves concentrating on surface structure, rather than meaning. Meaning becomes important when we focus on the process. After all, parents react as positively to the process, at least initially, as they do to the product. They view the fact that Janie is writing as more important that what Janie has written. Because successful parent models are seen to love reading and writing, whole language teachers ensure that children see them enjoying reading and writing.

Holistic teaching is based on the following basic principles:

— Language learning occurs in a social context that fosters and nurtures a love of listening, speaking, reading and writing.
— Adults are positive models for the learning.

— Language activities occur in both functional and meaningful contexts.

Theory in the Classroom

Reading is an interactive process that fortunate individuals learn early in life in high-literacy homes. Holistic classrooms emulate this environment by providing interactive language activities that integrate listening, speaking, reading and writing into literature and the study of content.

Classrooms like this are a joy to behold as children go about their independent learning tasks, tasks they often initiate on their own out of interest. It is their teacher's goal to promote meaningful experiences and provide activities that promote creative comprehension. This is also the goal of this book—to provide strategies that encourage creative comprehension.

Summary

So that's it, a little theory on which to base the design of programs and approaches for students. Using language is an interactive process in which human beings use the sources of information that are the most productive in particular situations. In the past, researchers limited readers' access to information, forcing them to rely, for example, on initial letters to recognize words because that's what was most efficient in the circumstances. Small wonder, then, that this showed only how adaptive human beings are rather than how we function in normal reading situations.

A more useful concept of language involves individuals gaining information or enjoyment from connected discourse, writing or speech. Advocates of a holistic approach view listening, speaking, reading and writing as integrated processes. They also view the classroom as an environment in which learning to read and write follows naturally from meaningful activities, not from the direct teaching of separate skills. Activities in holistic classrooms foster a love of reading and writing and emphasize process rather than product. The activities described in this book are based on this interactive views of language within the positive atmosphere of high-literacy classrooms.

. . . .

HOW MANY WEBS

DID CHARLOTTE SPIN?

Elementary teachers teach children to read and respond to good literature. Sometimes, however, reading instruction and responding to literature are confused by teachers who believe that the purpose of good books is to teach students to read. This is wrong. The purpose of good literature is to introduce students to different views and encourage them to appreciate different times and cultures, respond emotionally, come to know other individuals through text, consider and judge ideas, and use their imaginations. Some teachers do believe that students learn to read if they are introduced to good books and involved in literary activities. Indeed, learning to read may be a positive benefit of involvement in literary activities. This chapter begins by looking at reading as an interactive process.

Reading—An Interactive Process

Some language researchers refer to passages like the following as "texticles"—short, meaningless pieces of oral or written discourse used by university researchers to study language.

> Elizabeth was especially unruly that cold, frosty day in August as we trotted through the woods towards the big clearing near old lady Hansen's burned-out barn. I tried to coax her into a slower pace, but she was determined to have her way. I wondered why she was so anxious as she pulled away from me, putting pressure on my arm. Does were standing in the trail ahead of us. Bolting, they ran

into a thicket. The barn was black and rotting. I soon saw what had excited Elizabeth.

As you read this bit of prose, you probably envisaged a scene. Some readers visualize a rider on a horse, while others see someone walking a dog. Some sense evil omens, while others see an innocent walk in the woods with a spirited animal named Elizabeth. North American readers are often troubled by the reference to the cold August day because it doesn't match the familiar setting of their background script.

When we read, we engage in an interactive process, using our previous knowledge to create mental images of what's happening—unless, of course, it's a book about humanist epistemology or the hot-rolling of structural steel, content material that will be explored in a subsequent chapter.

Basal reading workbooks that require students to circle correct answers certainly don't foster this interactive reading process because they must focus on surface structure as they concentrate on getting the right answers. Many teachers convince themselves that the truth of a passage can be known by students if they, the teachers, guide students' comprehension by asking questions that encourage more than the literal-level recall of facts. But all this kind of questioning really does is place students' comprehension in the hands of teachers who may not know any better than students what's important enough to be comprehended. What does put comprehension in the hands of readers? A focus on active prediction.

The Directed Reading-Thinking Activity

In a 1971 article in *The Reading Teacher*, Russell Stauffer proposed that the typical reading lesson did not encourage students to use their natural abilities to make and confirm predictions as they read. He developed the directed reading-thinking activity (DRTA) to encourage students to develop and use this skill. The following version of the DRTA is one I've used successfully with native English-speaking and ESL students ranging from kindergarten to adult level.

Each student receives a copy of the material to be read, material they haven't seen before. They also receive an opaque sheet to cover portions of the text. Take care when selecting this sheet to make sure the print doesn't show through.

Students cover the first page, exposing only the sections indicated by the teacher. If they can't resist the temptation to peek ahead, the story can be displayed on an overhead transparency with selected parts shown. Or, if the material is photocopied, a paper cutter can be used to separate story segments.

During the DRTA, the teacher asks only three questions:

— What do you think this story is about?
— What do you think will happen next?
— What makes you think so?

While it's sometimes tempting to introduce other questions, it's important to ask only these three. Teachers who are concerned that students missed something essential can ask other questions once the DRTA is over.

Let's look at an example designed for older individuals. Begin by uncovering of the title:

Elliot Trimble's Frog Invasion

Students can read it silently or the teacher can read it aloud. Ask, "What do you think this story is about?" Follow up with, "What makes you think so?"

At this point, students' predictions are usually quite limited, especially if they are new to DRTAs. Adults who see this particular title often predict that the story is about an adventure in elementary school.

The next step is to uncover the author's name, if there is one, and ask the same questions. This may affect the predictions dramatically, depending on the extent of the children's background knowledge of an author. Think about how your own predictions might change if the author was revealed to be Hans Christian Andersen, Isaac Asimov or Agatha Christie.

Then, expose or invite students to expose more text. The amount exposed—not too little and not too much—is based on common sense.

Elliot Trimble's Frog Invasion
by
Eric von Slick

Elliot was trapped in the body of a ninety year-old, a body racked with the pains of age, oppressed by failing hearing and vision, abandoned by those who were family, isolated in a community of 400 old people. His walker leaned against the yellowing wall next to his bed. Its worn, black rubber handgrips had cracked from age and lack of use. Elliot's days were filled with talk, his own, talk unheard by others, his thoughts. He lectured himself. He spoke of the warm summer days of his youth, the feel of warmth on tanned arms, and a hundred other fading memories. He also spoke frequently of the frogs.

The questions now are:

— What do you think this story is about?
— What makes you think so?

Although we may have little direct experience with the thoughts and problems associated with people Elliot's age, we've likely thought about them and can empathize. We can create in our minds a script of the story, the roles of the various characters, and a million different scenes that could happen. Indeed, we may have formed some initial, personal feelings about Elliot. The next question, then, is vitally important:

— What do you think is going to happen next?
— What makes you think so?

It's at this point that some teachers are tempted to ask comprehension questions like, "What did Elliot think about?" because they're conditioned to follow procedures set out in teachers' guides or they know that comprehension isn't a simple process and want to make sure that students understand at different levels.

While concern about students' comprehension is legitimate, testing this is not the purpose of a DRTA. Indeed, I've observed that asking typical comprehension questions interferes with the process. It's therefore a good idea to save them until after the activity, for the post-DRTA discussions that are so interesting. If we analyze students' responses during a DRTA, it's clear that they do, in fact, comprehend text at all levels, without us interfering to ask "worksheetesque" questions. If you analyze your own thoughts about Elliot, for example, you'll likely realize that you understood the passage at several levels. You thought about it, re-creating Elliot and his environment in your imagination. This is the best kind of comprehension.

The DRTA progresses in stages until the story is finished. Often, students develop a kind of story anxiety as they work through the text. They want to read on, to find out the conclusion. One of the best features of DRTAs is that students become active, eager readers.

HOW CAN SHE DO A DRTA WHEN SHE CAN'T EVEN READ?

DRTAs can be adapted to take into account different needs and abilities. Non-readers, poor readers or those whose English is limited can still take part. Depending upon the students, a DRTA can be introduced through wordless picture books, a series of simple photographs or even cartoons. Because I can't draw at all, Thomas Peter Collins of Galileo High School in San Francisco volunteered to draw the following sketches for a writing study I conducted. There are always individuals in a school, including talented students, who are excellent artists, so don't overlook them as a source of DRTA material.

What do you think this story is about?
What makes you think so?

Very young students or those whose English is extremely limited are often nervous about answering these questions. In some cases, it's better to begin by simply asking them to describe the scene—"What do you see in this picture?"—then question them about what's happening—"What do you think this story is about?" It's important to be positive about every contribution. Comments and questions like, "That's interesting," or "What makes you think so?" encourage students. Your enthusiasm for their responses will motivate them to participate.

At this point, students' predictions will likely be fairly limited. Typical predictions about the previous sketch are, "It's about a boy who is going into a room," "It's about a man who goes into a room and sees a boxful of kittens," and "The boy sees a boxful of money and he's going to steal it." A typical answer to the question "What's going to happen next?" is, "He's going to look in the box."

Show the second picture and ask the two questions again.

What do you think will happen next?
What makes you think so?

The beauty of these pictures is that there really are no correct answers. Indeed, the drawings were designed to be as neutral as possible. At this point, observations usually involve the boy seeing a surprise. Students from seven to eighteen have predicted that the box holds money, stamps, gold, kittens, puppies, answers to the math exam, toys, etc. Asked what they think is going to happen next, they've predicted everything from, "He'll steal it," to "He'll look and leave it alone," and "He'll take something out of the box."

Because students may be disappointed when they see the last picture and discover that nothing much has happened, it's important to point out that they made predictions based on very little information. In fact, most of the information came from their own imaginations and background knowledge.

Once students are comfortable with this procedure, invite them to describe or narrate the scenes or actions taking place in longer illustrated texts. The focus on prediction requires students to establish a story script in their minds based on the visual information in the illustrations. This provides them with opportunities to develop their awareness of cause-and-effect relationships, story sequences, story outcomes, and illustrations as sources of story information.

Wordless picture books—the bibliography contains a list of some I recommend—make execellent DRTA material that can be used in many different ways to encourage students to make predictions. One teacher selects five or six illustrations representing scenes from the beginning middle and end of a book and invites eleven- and twelve-year-olds to fill in the gaps with their own illustrations and text explaining what's happening and what's going to happen. Students then compare their versions with the original.

The next step is to include written text and easily predicted "stories." Again, recommendations are found in the bibliography. One of my favorites for this is Patricia Hutchins' *One Hunter*. Combining visual cues in the illustrations with predictable text, this book is based on counting from one to ten and bridges the gap between wordless picture books and books with text. I've used it with preschoolers, adults, ESL secondary and university students, and non-English speaking senior citizens. In one forty-minute DRTA with *One Hunter*, one group of non-English-speaking adults learned to read and understand the meaning of eighteen English words!

Repetition of patterns, like the one in the following excerpt from *The Judge*, is a feature of many predictable books.

The Judge
An Untrue Tale Told by Harve Zemach

Please let me go, Judge.
I didn't know, Judge,
That what I did was against the law,
I just said what I saw.

A horrible thing is coming this way,
Creeping closer day by day.

Because this pattern recurs throughout the book, students learn it quickly and begin to chime in as the teacher reads aloud. DRTAs increase comprehension significantly, producing avid readers who enjoy making predictions as they read. They should not, however, become the sole guide for reading major works of literature.

While active prediction forms the basis of many activities that can help increase students' comprehension of content texts, many other comprehension activities can also be used. These are the focus of the next chapter. Before we get to them, however, let's look at how DRTAs can be extended into other areas.

OFF TO THE MOVIES

As noted earlier, some students find it difficult to make predictions for various reasons. Wordless books help them learn to use visual clues and predictable books help them use language clues. Some students, however, begin to focus solely on illustrations as the information source for making inferences. Some of the suggestions that follow will help them learn to make inferences without relying solely on visual clues.

Television and film characters and new toys are very influential in students' lives. One teacher takes advantage of this interest in movies in several ways. He views a film carefully beforehand, deciding what to feature and when to stop the action. When he screens the film for the children, he asks typical DRTA questions at each predetermined stopping point.

I watched one session designed to help nine- and ten-year-old ESL students produce and use future tense verbs. The movie selected was filled with much action and little dialogue. When he stopped the film the first time, the teacher demonstrated the process by telling what had happened so far and making several future tense predictions about what was going to happen. Then, at subsequent stopping points, he encouraged the children to do the same.

Films can be used to develop students' skills and abilities in many areas. Some caution must be exercised, however, because copyright laws vary. In some areas, for example, it is illegal to show a rented video to a class. It's a good idea to be aware of the laws in your jurisdiction. If it isn't possible to use rented videos in your classroom, encourage students to make their own. Teachers have successfully used video cameras to film students' own stories, which were then used DRTA-fashion with other students. A nine-year-old, for example, videotaped his big brother's birthday party, at which guests went skydiving. The afternoon, which was filmed in sequence, made a wonderful natural story. The subsequent DRTA was outstanding.

Still photographs and newspaper cartoons also inspire marvelous DRTAs. Taped stories can also be used. Another teacher I know records portions of stories in sequence and places them in the listening center. Students listen to a section and record what they think will happen next, then compare their versions with the teacher's. It often takes up to two weeks to reach the end. Some students, who are more comfortable with writing than they are with oral recordings, use the computer in their writing center to write the DRTA passages.

A Polaroid camera makes it possible to involve students in many different ways. Indeed, a small group can produce a story and photograph it in five to eight stills, which can then become DRTA primers. It's also possible for them to use props and photograph frames of the story a section at a time.

DRTAS AND DRAMA

Drama can help students of all ages improve their comprehension and enjoy a story. Arlo Jannssen's *Unusual Stories from Many Lands*, for instance, contains outstanding short stories from different cultures that have surprise endings.

In small groups or as a class, students are then invited to create a dramatization showing what they think will happen next—but not necessarily how they think the story will end. Props can be furnished by the teacher or improvised by students. The teacher monitors the dramas carefully, making notes about characterizations and story lines to help guide subsequent discussions. Once the dramatizations have been presented, discussions help clarify predictions and specify information students used to make them.

In her book, *Diagnostic Teaching of Reading*, Barbara Walker suggests that teachers follow up by inviting students to write the ending of the story, read their endings aloud, read the actual text, and then compare their endings with the original.

While students enjoy this technique for extending DRTAs through drama, careful teacher guidance is necessary because behavior can become frivolous.

Literary Appreciation

While students love DRTAs and other activities that involve DRTA-like sequences, these should be used in moderation. They use much cognitive energy and can be tiring, not to mention tiresome, if overused. It is possible to get too much of a good thing. Furthermore, DRTAs are not always appropriate—especially when good literature is involved.

THERE'S MORE TO LIFE THAN DRTAS

DRTAs produce critical readers, but not necessarily literary readers. All of *Charlotte's Web*, for example, should not be read DRTA-fashion. It's good literature to be appreciated as a whole.

As adults, we don't answer a series of questions about the books we read, either DRTA-fashion or as post-reading comprehension exercises. As teachers, some of us have adopted the wrong metaphor in approaching literature. We treat literature the way surgeons approach exploratory operations. First, we cut into the text, separating it into parts. Then we analyze the parts like pathologists looking for disease. There are better metaphors.

THE "LITERARY" DISCUSSION

It may be that the "literary club book discussion" is too formal for elementary students because it's too elitist, too loaded with pretentious comments about things like "the author's clever use of post-constructivist metaphor." Perhaps, as P. David Pearson suggested to delegates at a conference, we should adopt the Paris sidewalk cafe approach in which friends get together to talk about books. This suggestion makes some teachers nervous because it's hard to grade. But how do we assess a student's love for a particular book, or for literature in general?

Think about what we often ask students to do after they've finished reading a good book like *Charlotte's Web*—write a book report or answer questions in a workbook. We're incredibly creative when it comes to devising ingenious versions of book reports. I remember suggesting that students design book jackets, interview authors, write alternative endings, write diaries for the main characters, etc.

Students may enjoy these activities once or twice, but not every time they read a good book. I never did find out what the students in my class thought about Charlotte's death, her love and devotion for Wilbur, or life.

Summary

No student should ever be asked to answer worksheet questions about a good book. Asking nine-year-olds how many webs Charlotte spun after reading *Charlotte's Web* ruins the purpose of the story. Alas, the tradition of assigning students worksheets, or, perhaps worse, the dreaded book report, has resulted in hundreds of thousands of adults who don't enjoy reading books and, in fact, don't read books at all.

The teacher's role in engendering a love of reading is vital, for, in many respects, it will determine how students view literature throughout their lives. Be an active, avid reader yourself. Tell students about the book you're reading—why you like it, why you think the author is good, why you like the choice of characters, what you think about their motivations, what you think about the ending of the story, and why you recommend the book.

Give your book reports informally whenever you have time—while the class is walking to the gym, just after silent reading time, or during your regularly scheduled book report time. Encourage students to make similar reports of their own. Write brief comments in their logs about what you're reading and what they're reading. Let them know about your appreciation of different books and authors and how much you value their opinions about books they've read.

In the end, do we care if they know how many webs Charlotte spun? Not much.

. . . .

WHY, WHAT, WHEN, HOW?

Traditional approaches to reading instruction feature exercises designed to improve word recognition, vocabulary development and comprehension. This chapter outlines effective comprehension strategies based on an interactive model of language designed to be used in classrooms that emphasize the process, rather than the product, of reading and writing. While the activities are considerably more interesting than those found in typical reading workbooks, many of them do continue to place students' comprehension in the teacher's hands and should, therefore, be used sparingly.

Comprehension Levels

While reading authorities seem to disagree on just about everything, they tend to agree that there are three levels of comprehension—literal or detail, inferential, and critical and evaluative, sometimes called applicative. Because each relates to a different level of cognitive functioning, or thinking, teachers ask different kinds of questions to foster comprehension at the various levels.

Literal-level comprehension: Questions at this level require readers to supply answers based on information stated in text. Operating at the surface level, they aren't required to make inferences, other than low-level ones involving a knowledge of the syntactic and semantic conventions of English. For instance, literal-level comprehension is involved when a text reads, "John was very hungry. He ate three plates of spaghetti," and the question is, "Who ate three plates of spaghetti?" To answer the question with "John," readers must infer only that the pronoun "he" represents John. Because typical workbook questions often require little more than simple memory work, their chief virtue may be that they keep students quiet.

Inferential-level comprehension: At this level, readers deal with and understand the writer's ideas, thinking about the material they read. They can make generalizations about text, understand the writer's purpose, and anticipate and predict outcomes. In effect, they are able to go beyond the surface structure of the text and operate on meaning.

Critical and evaluative-level comprehension: Many reading authorities separate critical and evaluative, or applicative, comprehension. The term refers to readers' ability to evaluate and make critical judgments about their reading. They're able to evaluate whether a text is valid and expresses opinion rather than fact, as well as apply the knowledge gained from the text in other situations. "How would you judge the protagonist's quality of life?" is an evaluative question.

Unfortunately, because ensuring that questions require different levels of thought takes time, the tendency is to ask questions at the literal level because they're the easiest to make up.

Try making up some questions yourself. It's not easy to come up with higher level questions. Then think about "correcting" students' answers. It gets even more difficult!

Literal-Level Comprehension Strategies

This is the easiest level to measure because it's so straightforward. Answers are either right or wrong. The problem is that many teachers make incorrect assumptions about literal-level comprehension. We assume, for example, that this kind of comprehension is important in *all* cases. While it's certainly important to be able to read and remember details in order to follow a recipe, assemble a bicycle, or fill out a form, readers in real life are rarely asked to read a passage, then repeat the information from memory.

Our early-morning newspaper-reading ritual reveals the usual literal-level comprehension approach taken by adults.

We remember what's interesting or important and often forget the rest. We seldom encounter situations in which we are prohibited from returning to the text. Indeed, when we assemble a bicycle, for example, we read the instructions, re-read, re-re-read, and probably discuss and rehearse as the process unfolds. This is quite different from the typical classroom reading exercise in which students are asked questions without recourse to the original text.

Reading for details is almost always done for a purpose—to follow instructions or find a friend's house on a map. As teachers, many of us fail to understand that reading for details is nearly always motivated reading. As a result, the motivation we provide students in classrooms is often secondary and artificial. No wonder they view these exercises with despair.

Our appreciation of a story doesn't hinge on a knowledge of the details. Nevertheless, it's frustrating to know that I may base my estimation of your comprehension—the way you cognitively process a story, the way you think—on your ability to remember bits of inconsequential trivia.

Exercises emphasizing literal-level comprehension should involve material that's worth remembering. This judgment represents the most important consideration in reading education. I choose to believe that any literal-level comprehension questions are boring and it may be worth considering that there is no compelling reason for teachers to ask them about narrative texts at all, unless, of course, students have demonstrated a need to practice remembering.

This may leave us in a bit of a quandary about literal-level comprehension and our role as teachers, a quandary we'll consider in more detail in the material that follows. It delineates when, how, and with what material literal-level comprehension exercises should be designed and initiated. It also discusses strategies that can help improve the recall of details, and memory in general. Some students will always have trouble recalling facts worth remembering after they read them in a text. Our goal is to find ways of helping them improve their remembering strategies.

WALKING THE TEMPLE

"Walking the temple" is a strategy designed to help students remember details, visualize characters and make inferences.

It originated with Simonides, an inventor and prize-winning singer, who attended a banquet in 478 B.C. Simonides stepped outside for a moment to get a breath of air. While he was outside, the roof of the temple collapsed, killing or injuring the other guests. Simonides was able to remember accurately and report where every guest had been seated.

He did this by forming a mental picture of the room, then visualizing himself walking from pillar to pillar to remember each individual. Improving recall by creating mental images, the loci method, was adopted by orators to help them remember their presentations. Both Plato and Aristotle advocated using visual images to impress memory into the mind.

The word "loci" means "places" in Latin. The loci method involves associating the material to be remembered with places in a building or room. It's a form of mnemonics based on the notion that visualizing each locus provides a cue that triggers a series of mental images and their associated memories in the correct order. It's interesting to note that if I ask how many windows are in your house, you'll likely close your eyes and form a picture of the house in your mind, "walking" from room to room in your imagination and counting the windows as you go.

Training students to form mental images within the framework of a physical structure helps improve their memory. Begin with places students know well, like their rooms at home. Invite them to close their eyes and visualize their rooms. Direct them to start at the door, visualizing the walls one at a time, then begin to walk around looking at things in the room. They might get up one at a time and "walk" through their rooms, reporting to the class where they are and what's around them. Complete the activity with a sketch of the room as they visualized it in their mind's eye.

Then, try telling a simple story, one that takes place in two or three locations. Read the introduction aloud. Help students form mental image of the sites by encouraging them to close their eyes while you recount what they might visualize in each instance. You can even use the rooms and hallways of your own school. Ask yourself what items in each location would help readers remember the story?

Visualization helps readers remember details, visualize characters and make inferences. The role of visualization in reading comprehension will be considered later.

Inferential-Level Comprehension Strategies

Inferential-level comprehension involves readers in thinking about what they've read and coming to conclusions that go beyond the information given in the text.

In this section, we'll steer clear of the typical approach to measuring comprehension, which involves constructing, duplicating and handing out a series of questions on worksheets, and focus on strategies that are less teacher-directed.

DRAWING CONCLUSIONS

To make inferences, we must be able to draw conclusions from descriptors set out in a text. Some students, especially those who rely on illustrations to help them make inferences, have difficulty doing this when there are no pictures.

Try reading the following:

> It was July and the hillsides were white and the air was cool. It was six in the morning and the cattle were heading for the pastureland just south of the creek. As Jennifer walked down the road, she thought about the green grass of the pasture.

Here is a variety of conclusions that can be drawn from this brief passage:

— It was unseasonably cold ("It was July…the hills were white and the air was cool").

— It was somewhere in the southern hemisphere, maybe Australia ("It was July…the hills were white and the air was cool…she thought about the green grass…").

— It was Australia and Jennifer was driving the cattle to the pasture ("It was July…the hills were white and the air was cool…she thought about the green grass…").

— It was Australia and Jennifer was a cow walking to the pasture with the rest of the cattle early in the morning ("It was July…the hills were white and the air was cool. It was six in the morning…she thought about the green grass…").

— It was southern California and, in the cool morning, Jennifer, a cow, was walking with the other cattle past hills of white sand in the desert to an irrigated pasture.

For students who have trouble making inferences or drawing conclusions, it's essential to make the process explicit. This can be done by helping them draw conclusions from a single context-rich sentence like the following:

> The man in the blue coat held up his hand and stopped the traffic.

Invite students to read this sentence, then ask, "What is this about? What makes you think so?" If they have trouble, ask them to describe the individual and draw a sketch. If all else fails, explain the logical conclusions explicitly:

— The man has on a blue coat.
— He holds up his hand and stops traffic.
— The man is a police officer (because police officers wear blue uniforms and control traffic by making signals with their hands).

As students become more confident, they can move on to increasingly complex paragraphs, like the following:

> Bob likes to swim up the river and back. His favorite place is just under the bridge. He's been swimming every day since he was born. His mother also likes to swim. A man caught his mother in a net and took her away.
>
> Bob is a _____.

Keep in mind that, as the paragraphs become more interesting, it's possible to base many different—but equally logical—inferences on the same material, as indicated by the number of conclusions drawn from the earlier paragraph about Jennifer, who may or may not have been a cow.

BACKGROUND KNOWLEDGE

The inferences we make and conclusions we draw from a particular text depend, in large part, on our background. This is a valuable point to make with students. Background knowledge is a powerful part of our comprehension mechanism. For a long time, teachers have known that students' comprehension improves when they're able to apply their own background knowledge to help them understand what they read. While procedures for encouraging them to do this have many names and variations, the best-known may be Kathryn

Au's experience-text-relationship (ETR) lesson, a model she used when teaching multicultural students.

A text is selected, usually by the teacher, and the background is analyzed carefully. It's often most effective to discuss the background within the framework of introducing the characters and setting of the story.

Let me describe a basic lesson plan that divides instruction into story segments. The first stage introduces the background of the story through teacher-directed discussion, photographs, artifacts, movies and so on. Often, the best kind of background knowledge is acquired through actual field trips. Kathryn Au called this the experience phase.

Once the background is established, the first portion of the story is read and the knowledge developed by the teacher is discussed and related to the text. Children are invited to make predictions about what is likely to happen next. Au called this the text phase. The story is continued in this fashion, alternating between prediction, discussion and silent reading.

The relationship phase of an ETR lesson returns students' attention to the background-developing discussions and provides them with an opportunity to talk about what they learned while reading the story. The lesson concludes with a summary of the story by the teacher or, if possible, the students.

Helping students relate what they already know to what they are reading is a key element of ETR lessons. The teacher must make certain that students have enough information to understand a story. If they don't, they won't comprehend it, other than on a surface level.

The activities presented so far are designed for students who need help with some basic processes. The following are more general and more independent comprehension strategies.

STORY STRUCTURE

One fairly non-directive technique, suitable for nearly all students, involves a sequence of steps—read, visualize (think about the story and its characters), sketch and report.

Students think about the story, using their background knowledge and the loci method to visualize the settings, then sketch a picture or series of pictures that represent their understanding of the story and characters. They needn't worry about the quality of their artwork—they can use stick figures if they wish.

While this activity is a good way to measure students' comprehension of a story, it tends to focus on story sequence and details unless teachers encourage students to think about the characters. Depending on students' needs and abilities and the objectives of the activity, the final step—the report—can be presented orally in a conference, recorded on tape, or written in a log book or on the sketch itself. Whatever form the report takes, it should be dated and saved, perhaps in a portfolio containing other work samples and assessment items (see the chapter titled "Is an 'A' by Any Other Name as Sweet?").

The beauty of this strategy cannot be overstated. It is a simple, effective assessment procedure, especially if the report is attached. It helps readers work out character relationships, make inferences and remember details, especially if they also understand the loci method and use it to help construct a sketch. I've used it with ESL students who comprehend stories but lack the basic English ability to construct answers to my contrived questions. Indeed, their sketches often reveal vocabulary items that can be taught in later lessons.

Despite its simplicity, some students may have trouble with this strategy, needing guidance to use visualization and sketching in a systematic way. This can be done by providing a framework, in the form of a visualization map, that helps students make inferences.

Visualization mapping is based on the notion that children's stories tend to share a common abstract structure, sometimes called the story grammar. Included in this structure are items like the initial setting, introduction of main characters, the theme, and the resolution of the problem. Research indicates that children as young as six have internalized the elements of a story, often representing these simply as the beginning, middle and end.

The visualization map begins with a frame designed to include a sketch of the setting and characters. The problem with using strategies based on the notion of story grammar, however, is that relatively few stories conform exactly to the model. Students will learn to create their own maps after they've experienced stories that don't match the prototype.

Once students are confident about using sketches to map stories, encourage them to complete the activity without creating the pictures on a form.

A dramatic, visual way to demonstrate that stories have different significant parts is to invite students to listen to or read a story. Then ask each to think about—and sketch—the most memorable part. When their sketches are complete, invite them to form a group and display their pictures on a table. Whenever I've asked a group of ten or more students to try this, the complete story has been represented in their pictures.

Learning about visualization mapping and story grammar helps students internalize an understanding that stories have a structure and this understanding improves their comprehension.

CHARACTER ANALYSIS

While the suggestions that follow tend to place control in the hands of teachers, they do, nevertheless, help students develop their ability to make inferences by encouraging them to read more creatively.

The first involves rating a series of statements about a story on a scale. Here's an example:

1. Lorraine Bass was a good mother who loved her son.

Agree   Disagree

because _____

Invite students to indicate with an X where their thinking is. Do they strongly agree with the statement? Strongly disagree? Or does their opinion fall somewhere in between the two extremes?

It's worth remembering that the inferences statements like this require students to make may be significant—or they may not. Because the teacher selects the statements, the teacher controls the inferences students make.

Depending upon students' needs and abilities, teachers can vary this activity by writing a statement on the chalkboard or an overhead transparency just after the information needed to make the inference has been read, thereby showing explicitly how inferences are made.

Activities like this help improve students' comprehension. The "because" portion of the activity is essential, as is a teacher-led discussion of the responses, for it is at this stage that students are encouraged to talk about their thinking with respect to each statement.

Teachers can also select several events from a story and invite students to create a bar graph showing, for example, how happy a particular character was at the specified point. Different colors can be used to include several individuals on the same graph. While this is a fairly sophisticated activity, very young students can learn to do it quite easily with a bit of group instruction. Older students can be invited to read and determine for themselves the character traits they wish to infer, an effective way of assessing comprehension.

During the 1950s and '60s, when teachers discovered how important social perceptions are in classrooms and set about learning who liked whom and who would like to be whose friend, the sociogram was invented. A sociogram—it isn't necessary to use this name—helps teachers discover how students understand characters and their roles in a story.

A sociogram is a kind of specialized map. Recently, visuals that look something like sociograms have been used to teach vocabulary and comprehension. These are called semantic webs, semantic maps or webs. Researchers have found that students' comprehension and learning improve when they generate illustrative materials such as semantic webs.

If students have difficulty creating a web for an entire story, they might begin by focusing on vocabulary. Take the word "dog," for instance, and construct a web on the chalkboard, asking students to volunteer words. The following "dog" web was created by a group of eight- and nine-year-olds.

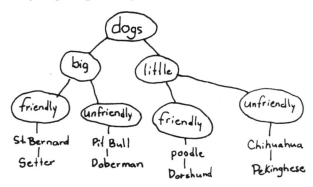

Webbing combines visualization and understanding of story relationships, often revealing that students understand extremely complicated relationships. Webs can focus on cause-and-effect relationships, sequence, character and story elements. While webbing focuses on inferential-level comprehension, it can also reveal a great deal about students' literal- and critical-level comprehension of a story.

Critical and Evaluative-Level Comprehension

The strategies described in the previous sections not only foster literal- and inferential-level comprehension but also develop students' ability to think critically and make judgments. This is, in many respects, the most interesting and enjoyable aspect of comprehension because readers can, in many cases, freely express their own opinions about text.

Critical and evaluative comprehension entails making judgments about the actions, characters, reliability, validity, notions, opinions, statements and ideas presented in a text. How does a reader know what is propaganda or opinion rather than fact? How does a reader judge the worth of a particular viewpoint?

I've often heard people say things like, "You know, they say that fluorescent lighting causes cancer," because they read it somewhere and didn't question the source. Students need to be encouraged to ask questions about the material they read. Is an author writing to convince readers that her view is right or correct? If so, does she have credibility? Is her viewpoint valid? Is it biased? These and other critical reading skills are absolutely essential when reading materials such as social studies texts, newspapers and magazines. Strategies for developing these skills in relation to content material are discussed in the next chapter.

Critical reading skills are also important when reading literature. However, requiring students to answer workbook-style questions designed to promote these skills is to be avoided. The typical questions related to literature—Is the story believable? Was the plot a good one? Was the conclusion appropriate? Were the characters believable within the context of the story?—are usually best reserved for formal literature study classes, the kind found in universities.

The development of critical thinking is a natural consequence of students' intimate contact with stories that are meaningful and enjoyable in an atmosphere that encourages the love of literature and reading. The teacher's model is the foundation upon which students' attitudes towards reading will be formed.

When we present our own book-reading activities to the group, we can make statements like, "I thought the characters in this book were very realistic and the author's choice of words painted vivid pictures of them for me." When students emulate this model, we have an opportunity to evaluate their critical and evaluative comprehension. This approach is discussed further in the section of the following chapter titled "Literary Appreciation."

Although critical and evaluative comprehension should be developed, it should not necessarily be taught in the traditional sense. Students become critical readers by participating in activities that foster reading independence.

LOG BOOKS

Some teachers are troubled by the idea that traditional workbook exercises may be detrimental to students' reading development because these activities are widely used and expected by many individuals, including other teachers, principals, parents and, yes, the students themselves. Written workbook exercises, however, are not the only way of providing a written record of students' progress.

Ships' captains and aircraft pilots use log books to keep notes about their ships, their trips, their crews, their passengers, and events that occur. The log is a chronicle of the professional life of a sea captain or airline pilot, one required by law. It contains both professional and personal comments. In the same way, students' logs chronicle the lives of individuals occupied by the joy of learning. They contain their thoughts about what they're reading, what they're learning, what they're doing, and how they feel about it.

Is it unreasonable to expect six-year-olds to maintain logs? Not if they have written from the first day of school so that they view writing as something they can do, something that brings them satisfaction. Jon Shapiro, a colleague at the University of British Columbia, and I have been astounded by young children's eagerness to write. We've seen six-year-old ESL students happily write thirty-page entries in their logs.

Older students from traditional classrooms, however, often react negatively to attempts to initiate log-writing. They tend to view writing as drudgery designed to create a product that is returned to them filled with red marks and the admonition to improve things like spelling and paragraph construction. Keeping a log, however, is a different kind of writing experience, the essence of which is process and meaning rather than product.

A log book normally speaks to one person—the one who does the writing. In classrooms, the audience for a log should be the person who writes it. The teacher is a bystander granted the privilege of reading students' thoughts. The log is inviolable—the teacher may *never* correct it in the traditional sense.

There is some debate about what a log should look like. Some have blank pages, some pages that are half blank and half lined, and some pages that are completely lined. Many teachers designate a regular time each day for log-writing, often during the last period, when students can reflect on the day's activities. There are several variations on log books.

The learning log: This is the pure form of the log, a diary in the truest sense. In it, students write their thoughts about what they've done, what they're going to do, how they think they've progressed, what they have and haven't liked about what they've done, what they think they've learned, and what they wish to learn. The teacher monitors the log, keeps separate notes, and talks to individual students about their entries—privately, of course. Even six-year-olds are capable of maintaining logs like this, as the following entry illustrates:

I Am goweing To sor
AND Biy Som miik
mak Hot chocLet

In most cases, teachers maintain a master log, usually a loose-leaf binder divided alphabetically so that separate notes can be kept for each student. At the end of every day, they collect and read the students' logs and makes notes in the master log. These notes are unbelievably informative.

Student-teacher cooperative logs: Some teachers choose to write brief notes directly in the students' logs, often on the inside back cover where they are less intrusive. Others opt to maintain cooperative logs. In this case, students write entries and the teacher responds every day. Here's an example:

> i red the story bout big egle the indian warior today and i like it so much.
>
> I'm glad you liked the story about Big Eagle. I have another book about Indians I hope you will read. See me tomorrow and I will give it to you.

You may despair at the prospect of reading and writing in thirty-or-so log books every night. It *is* an onerous task, but no more so than correcting a pile of worksheets. Cooperative logs put teachers in close touch with individual students. They provide us with an opportunity to do far more than simply monitor daily activities. If we respect their privacy and develop students' trust that they can write whatever they wish, logs give us insights into their progress, needs, successes and personal problems. They become indispensable to comprehension instruction.

Log Books and Reading Comprehension

When they first begin keeping logs, many students are uncertain about what to write. The teacher's role is to guide them into recording their thoughts about school and their learning, though almost anything is acceptable. Some teachers actively guide students by posting lists of suggestions. These might include a list of finished and unfinished activities, things students would like to do, things they're happy—or unhappy—about, and so on.

Primary students who find writing difficult can be encouraged to include sketches of, for example, a story accompanied by a brief comment and perhaps a happy or sad face showing their reaction. Some teachers print a series of sentence stems like the following on a bulletin board for students to copy and fill in either a sketch or a word or phrase.

_____ was the main character and I think he was

_____.

_____ was a book that I think is

_____.

I felt _____ about _____.

Sentence stems are only temporary models for students who are hesitant about writing in their logs. In fact, many teachers view them negatively because they impose the teacher's model on students' writing. In my experience, nearly all students enjoy writing if it has been part of their program since they began school.

Older students often write a great deal. The following is an eleven-year-old's log entry:

I wrote a letter to the President today because you suggested it to me. I don't think he will write back. Today I finish Gentlehands by Kerr. It made me so sad because Buddy had a grandfather who was so kind and gentle and he loved him so much. But he turned out to be a criminal who did some bad things in a war a long time ago. People killed his dog and called him a Nazi dog. I'm so sad about the story because Buddy lost his grandfather and he lost all the good feelings he had for him because he found out the truth about him being bad. I also not feeling too happy because I tried the arithmetic examples you gave me. Please help me with the percent problems I get lost with all the zeroes. I feel sad because the book and because of Buddy. Buddy love his grandpa so much and I know his feelings must be black now. Do every older people have secrets they keep from people who love them?

Clearly this child comprehended the story, *Gentlehands*, at many different levels and was able to make critical judgments about her reading. To ask her to fill out a worksheet would be a crime. Students who maintain logs develop a wonderful metacognitive ability. They're able to talk about and react to their reading and learning. And, through conferences or written responses, teachers can probe their comprehension of texts in marvelous, non-intrusive ways.

An important ingredient in holistic classrooms, logs are discussed further in the chapter titled "Keeping the Warehouse in Order."

If you're still convinced that students should be asked to do traditional reading comprehension work to ensure that they master the important skills, let me suggest that we offer them choice, that activities be available for those who wish to do them. It's surprising how many will choose to do these activities when they're not required to. An eight-year-old in one of my classes loved to work on the programmed readers I found in the school storeroom. She liked circling correct answers in a text. I'm convinced that she felt a real sense of satisfaction when she finished a workbook. As teachers, we should offer students the opportunity to explore activities that interest them. If we're good at what we do, the activities can be enjoyable and students will learn.

Reading and reading activities should not become drudgery. Our goal in designing activities to accompany the reading program is to make them attractive and enjoyable so students will be motivated to do them. Fortunately, evidence suggests that students' literal-level comprehension develops even when the focus is on higher-level comprehension activities.

Setting up activity centers in the classroom is one way to accommodate a variety of needs, interests and abilities. Try to include some of the following activities, which can be adapted and used in a thousand different forms:

— Students change the form of the reading so that a poem becomes a story, a story becomes a play, etc.
— Students become newspaper reporters and record the story on an audiotape. The teacher checks students' versions to assess whether they have comprehended the story and can distinguish relevant from irrelevant facts.
— Students create a game based on a story. The stages of the game are based on the events in the story.
— Give students a story without the ending and ask them to write one, then compare their endings with the author's, judging which is more plausible, realistic, etc.
— Students produce drawings that represent the story.
— Students create and present a play based on the events and characters of a story.
— Students play the role of characters from a story who are being interviewed for a TV show.

— Set up a "What's My Line?" show in which classmates question individual students about a role they assume. For instance, someone who has read a story about space travel might assume the role of a space traveler and answer questions based on the material in the story.

In addition to being enjoyable, activities like these help students develop some of the skills and strategies teachers may believe are important and might not be learned independently. They also provide evidence that students are learning to comprehend.

Summary

If we look around at the readers we see as we walk through a park or sit on a bench in a mall, we see people who are reading because they enjoy it. In a bank or office, we see people reading because they're looking for important information. If we look at the readers in a traditional classroom, however, they're likely reading because they must in order to answer questions in a workbook or on a worksheet when they finish.

This chapter has presented activities and strategies designed to help students comprehend text—and enjoy reading. This should be every teacher's goal. The activities don't represent a comprehensive program. The chapter titled "Keeping the Warehouse in Order" discusses how these activities can be integrated into a broader classroom program.

A good reading program excites students and nurtures their ability to use language in creative and meaningful ways. Creative reading comprehension activities compel students to read more because they're interested. It makes them lifelong lovers of reading. As a rule, it's a good idea to avoid asking literal-level comprehension questions about narrative material. As teachers, we care that students *want* to read. That's what this chapter has been about.

. . . .

THE SQUARE OF THE

HYPOTENUSE EQUALS...

Many content subject teachers believe that reading instruction happens only in the primary grades. While we should certainly be worried about students learning content in subjects like math, social studies, science and health, we should also be concerned about reading because the sad truth is that many older students fail to learn from the material they read because they don't know how to read to learn. This chapter emphasizes using interactive reading processes to learn content. It opens with an examination of teachers' responsibility for assessing what's worth teaching, then moves on to discuss how prediction can be used in content reading.

Why Is Content Reading So Hard?

You probably know at least one eight-year-old who's an expert in something. In my case, the eight-year-old is a boy who knows more about dinosaurs than anyone I've met. He knows their technical names, their sizes, their habitats, their distribution and their eating habits. Merely mentioning the word dinosaur brings a sparkle to his eyes. Yet, this same child has trouble reading and remembering about the westward expansion that occurred in Canada during the 1800s or about community people and resources.

Content teachers expect students to read texts and answer questions about their reading. Can you remember your own school days—and the hours you spent reading social studies texts, for instance? How much of the material—the dates, people and issues—do you remember? Reading social studies is difficult for many students because they consider it irrelevant. Much of the material we expect them to read is written so that at least 30 to 50 per cent of a class has difficulty comprehending it.

The textual features students encounter in content material are quite different from those in the stories they're more familiar with. Features that make content material more difficult than stories are:

— More complex sentence structures.
— More difficult non-concrete and specialized vocabulary that may include non-standard meanings for familiar words (e.g., "conductor" in a science class means something different from "conductor" in a music class).
— More abstract material.
— Different kinds of visual aids, such as graphs, maps, charts and time lines.
— The introduction of more new concepts.
— Text that is more "information-packed" and material that is more "concentrated."
— A wider variety of writing styles.

While reading these texts may be difficult, teachers sometimes use strategies that make it even more difficult. In some cases, the way we teach almost guarantees that students will forget nearly everything they read. For example, what do you remember about South America from your elementary school social studies classes? My most vivid memories involve a papier-mâché relief map of South America I helped make. The annual value of Brazil's coffeee exports now escapes me, but I have a good sense of the size of the country and where the rivers, jungles and mountains are. This knowledge came from the activity, not from the books I read.

Content teachers are a little like smorgasbord cooks who prepare thousands of items in the hope that every guest will be able to find something that appeals. This metaphor is unfortunate. It's demoralizing to think that we may be spending thousands of hours filling students' heads with facts and figures they're certain to forget.

Most of us believe that some material is difficult to read because we aren't expert enough to understand it. Students, for example, often believe that physics is difficult to read because the average reader isn't smart enough to comprehend what is written. The average reader seems to believe that specialists are able to read technical material in their field, text that she can't understand because it's too difficult, in much the same way that she might read a novel. Yet in an article in *Journal of Reading*, Jeffrey Mallow pointed out that even physicists must slow down, make notes in the margins, reread and reconsider articles about physics. He concluded, "Readers seem to relinquish their powers of judgment when confronted with science texts. They assume, often erroneously, that their failure is due to their lack of competence. It may well be that the writing is obscure."

Do I Really Want to Know That...?

The first judgment we should make about content material concerns what is worth teaching—and what isn't.

Sometime during the nineteenth century, one-room schoolhouses with their family groupings began to disappear. Schools became warehouse-like buildings, with many small rooms designed to hold students related by age or accomplishment.

The stratified warehousing of students resulted in fixed rows of immovable desks, "wardenesque" control of their behavior, military-like scheduling of lessons, attention to rote learning, and indifference to variations in their interests, abilities, needs, skills, talents, backgrounds, capabilities and motivations. In fact, the classroom of the twentieth century seemed designed to house the maximum number of students in the smallest possible space, thereby restricting movement, curtailing the natural human predisposition to communicate, and creating a nearly impossible learning environment for teachers and students. For a hundred years or so, we've taught students in assembly-line fashion the million or so facts that have been mandated by superintendents, legislation and curriculum guides and committees.

Incredibly, researchers invaded these educational warehouses and attempted to identify the characteristics of teachers who seemed to perform best in these deplorable circumstances. They developed a number of mechanistic formulas to describe what they called "effective" teachers.

Teacher effectiveness programs—promising to make the teaching of the thousands of facts and figures mandated by curriculum guides more efficient—were invented, packaged, given cute acronyms, and sold to hundreds of thousands of teachers across North America.

In my view, classrooms are more than production lines. They are environments inhabited by human beings who think, feel, act, react and learn. Teachers must be more than robots, mechanically teaching a sequence of skills. Teachers produce profound changes in students' attitudes, characters, mores, and perceptions of the world. We influence students to expand their perceptions of their own abilities and unique characteristics, to make lifelong choices, to form attitudes, biases and beliefs. We should ask not whether teachers can become better and more efficient at teaching the skills they are asked to teach but, rather, are these skills worth teaching?

We have all been both students and teachers. At one time or another, we've probably all complained because we've been required to learn something and recall it on a test, then forgotten it within hours. Was this learning worth the time and effort? Was the information we crammed and then forgot worth knowing in the first place? Are our lives better today because we can remember that the square of the hypotenuse of a right-angled triangle is equal to the sum of the squares of the other two sides?

What Everyone Should Know

As teachers, we should consider carefully what we teach. The following table outlines six essential components of knowledge:

A Knowledge Matrix

	Know That	Know How
Must		
Should		
Want to		

This table classifies knowledge into two categories: "know that" and "know how." The "know that" category represents basic knowledge of facts or reality. Electricity kills, London is in England, Washington is the capital of the USA, and water is wet are examples of the kind of knowledge that might be placed in this category. The "know how" category represents things like knowing how to swim, drive a car, make bread, and read, the last being of the utmost importance to us, let's hope. As teachers, we're concerned with both categories of knowledge—but in three different ways:

— Knowledge students "must" acquire.
— Knowledge students "should" acquire (for a good reason, we believe).
— Knowledge students "want to" acquire.

The matrix could be expanded to include categories such as "shouldn't know that" (as judged by someone) and "mustn't know how," but these will not be discussed here. The question teachers must ask is, Is this worth knowing?

Students "must" know some basic things, such as their telephone numbers, that electricity is dangerous, that fire burns, how to put on a dress or pants, how to tie their shoes (or fasten Velcro), and how to cook. As teachers, we share responsibility for teaching items in this category with other individuals, such as parents. By and large, it's primary teachers who shoulder the burden of ensuring that students learn these things, sometimes called readiness or survival skills.

Reading is a skill that many primary teachers believe falls into this category. They may be right, but that's debatable. Teachers of older students, too, instruct them in areas that they "must" know. It may be that teaching social conventions and responsibilities is an integral part of this task.

Even broader than the "must" know category is what students "should" know. Most of what we teach falls into this category. Someone somewhere decided that students should know how many senators there are, who the first prime minister was, how many eggs make up a dozen, how to tell time, how to balance a checkbook, and how to find a number in the telephone book. Of course, many people eke out a fairly happy existence without knowing how to do a lot of things we think they "should."

Finally, some students "want to" know the names of all the aircraft used in World War II, the batting averages of the St. Louis Cardinals, the names of all the rap groups in California, how to operate a computer, how to make realistic line drawings or how to repair automobiles.

Deciding what "must" be learned and what "should" be learned is a daunting task for teachers. As professionals, we have several options:

— We can assume that our curriculum guides accurately identify important information.
— We can assess our curriculum guides and determine what *we* think is important for students to learn.
— We can independently identify items we consider important to learn.
— We can evaluate the lives of our students and identify information that appears important for them to learn. An added burden is deciding when and in what order to teach the identified knowledge.

Don't panic. I'm not suggesting that you come up with an integrated curriculum. The purpose of the knowledge matrix is simply to provide a method of identifying material in written text that must or should be taught to students and, by exclusion, material that should not. By treating everything that appears in textbooks as material that *should* be taught, we risk trivializing material that shouldn't be trivialized and aggrandizing material that may be trivial.

THE B-29 BOMBER

Material that students want to learn automatically becomes meaningful to them. When I was teaching a class of seven- and eight-year-olds, one child fell in love with B-29 bombers. He made models, read books, did research and, today, some fifteen years later, still has an abiding interest in them.

Our pivotal task, as teachers, is to discover students' interests, search out materials for them and equip them to search out materials independently. Finding out what they like to read is fairly easy, but it's something that's seldom done.

The quickest—and most direct—way to discover students' interests is to ask. With the class assembled as a group, the following typical assessment scene might take place:

Teacher: I like stories about human beings who struggle with big problems. I've just finished reading a book by Robert Cormier that tells the story of a boy who's dying of cancer. It's an interesting—and sometimes sad—tale about a boy who has to face death. I'm also interested in photography, zoology and traveling in places like Greece. Tell me, David, what are you interested in and what have you read lately?

David: I read a comic book about the lost lagoon. I like to read about transformers, robots, teenage mutant ninja turtles, and all kinds of science stuff about space.

As each student speaks, the teacher records on a class list notes about their interests and recent reading activities. Many students will have read little other than school texts, so it may take some probing to find out about their interests. Once these are recorded, they can be categorized to identify interest groups. The following is a portion of a chart completed after an interest survey was conducted:

	Medicine	Dinosaurs	Snakes	Fashion
Paul		✓		
Edward			✓	
Tyrone			✓	
Martha				✓
Pamjit	✓			

The interest survey is used to begin selecting materials and to match students and materials. If you teach a large class, you may wish to try a written survey. Be cautious about doing so, however, because students may view it as another assignment. Oral surveys are more flexible because students' sub-interests and so on can be pursued. A graduated scale like the following can be used to design a group interest inventory:

Interest Inventory

1. When reading about dinosaurs, I feel:

   Very Happy   Happy   Neither   Unhappy   Very Unhappy

2. When reading about women's sports, I feel:

   Very Happy   Happy   Neither   Unhappy   Very Unhappy

3. When reading about insects, I feel:

   Very Happy   Happy   Neither   Unhappy   Very Unhappy

4. When reading, I feel:

   Very Happy   Happy   Neither   Unhappy   Very Unhappy

5. When reading my social studies textbook, I feel:

   Very Happy   Happy   Neither   Unhappy   Very Unhappy

The last two items are included as examples of other attitudes about reading that can be measured on a scale like this. Items relating to oral reading, reading in front of a class, book reports, etc. can also be included. The results of an oral interest inventory can be used to identify items that can be included in a subsequent written inventory designed to gain insights into the interests students have in common and those that individuals may not have identified orally.

It's worth noting that serendipity also plays a role in discovering students' interests. The child who developed the passion for B-29s became interested after seeing a book about them on a visit to our school library. He asked for more material and I searched it out.

Teachers interested in finding out more about students' feelings about reading might invite them to complete a questionnaire like the following:

1. When I read aloud to the class, I feel...
2. When I'm at home reading for fun, I feel...
3. When I hear my teacher reading out loud, I feel...
4. When I hear my friends read aloud, I feel...
5. When I'm doing my math work, I feel...
6. When I do my reading worksheets, I feel...
7. When my teacher asks me to read aloud, I feel...
8. On my way to school, I feel...
9. When my friends hear me read aloud, they feel...
10. When my mother hears me read aloud, she feels...
11. When my teacher hears me read aloud, she feels...
12. When I read about science, I feel...

13. When I read social studies, I feel...
14. When I read math, I feel...
15. When someone gives me a book, I feel...
16. When I get my homework back from the teacher, I feel...
17. When I get my report card, I feel...
18. When my mother gets my report card, she feels...
19. When I'm reading silently to myself, I feel...
20. When I come to a new word that I don't know, I feel...

What Students Should Know

Teachers must make judgments about the material in texts. The underlying theme of this chapter is that in order to be productive, contributing members of society, there are some things we "must" know and others we "should" know.

After surveying a number of science books designed for use by nine- and ten-year-olds, I invented the following table of contents:

1 **Nutrition**

Food	Carbohydrates
Fats	Chemicals
Proteins	Vitamins and Minerals
Water	Food Requirements
Health	

2 **The Human Body**

Cells	Tissues
Organs and Systems	The Skeleton
The Muscles	The Nerves

3 **The Needs of the Body**

The Digestive System	The Respiratory System
The Circulatory System	The Nervous System

4 **Communities of Living Things**

The Forest	The Desert
The Seashore	The Ocean
The Pond	The Backyard

5 **Energy**

Heat	Light
Electricity	Sound
Chemical	

6 **Environmental Concerns**

Pollution   Extinction
Recycling   Noise Pollution
Heat Pollution   Ecology

Based on a scan of this table of contents, what information in this imaginary science book would you say students *must* know? To get a better idea, the next step would be to leaf through the book and see what the material looks like. This would help determine what should be taught and what must be learned.

For most teachers, the "must learn" category represents knowledge students really can't do without. This text probably contains some material that falls into this category. A lot of the material, however, focuses on things students *should* know to live a fuller life and become informed, contributing members of society and the world community. This may include knowledge about the human body, ecology, energy, nutrition and food. In addition, interest surveys may have revealed that the book contains material students *want* to know about.

I've decided to focus on the section containing information about life in the desert, mostly because it includes interesting material for students who live in my part of the world. To do this, I could very easily create a traditional study guide consisting of teacher-produced questions students are required to answer as they read. While study guides—which are discussed in the section of the next chapter titled "But Can She Read Independently?"—certainly help students read and comprehend text, they tend to prescribe what should be learned. There are useful and creative alternatives to this approach.

What Do We Already Know?

Teachers often fail to take advantage of information readers already possess. Brainstorming helps us—and the students— tap into this important knowledge source.

For example, if we were going to read a passage about scorpions as part of the unit on life in the desert, I might start by handing out a kind of pre-reading worksheet like the following:

Scorpions

Before reading... I know/expect that:	After reading... I didn't know/expect that:

I would then invite small groups of students to brainstorm information to include in the left column. (If the students in your class have trouble working in groups, read "Basketball Is a Nice Game" on page 92 before going any farther.) It's usually most efficient to appoint or ask the groups to select a secretary to record the items. In addition, a timer can be selected to help the group stay on task and finish within the time limit. If students have trouble, the teacher can model the process for the class by writing their ideas on an overhead transparency.

As the groups are working and especially when the activity is first introduced, it's vital for the teacher to circulate and eavesdrop on their conversations. Students are often hesitant to mention their ideas, possibly because they might be wrong. If I find that there is a lull in the flow of ideas, I might say something like, "I heard the group over here say that scorpions are nocturnal. What does that mean?" This usually encourages the flow to start again.

You might try this exercise yourself by taking a few minutes to jot down as many items as you can about scorpions. Then, compare your ideas with the following, taken from lists compiled by groups of adults.

I know or expect to read that:
— scorpions are spiders
— scorpions are insects
— they have six legs
— they have eight legs
— female scorpions eat their mates
— they can't cross a ring of fire
— Scorpions is the name of a heavy-metal group

- they live in deserts
- they hide in shoes and boots
- they live in jungles
- they have exoskeletons
- they are nocturnal
- they are invertebrates
- they have segmented bodies
- they are brown
- they are black
- they are yellow
- they are about an inch long
- their venom is fatal
- they have pincers
- they are in the lobster family
- they sting with their tails curved over their head
- black scorpions are an evil omen (Hong Kong)
- powdered small brown scorpions are an aphrodisiac
- scorpions live under rocks
- they scurry
- they are dropped into the shirts of unsuspecting tourists in Mexico

It's worth noting that when groups of elementary students are invited to do the same exercise, they, too, come up with many of these ideas. How does your list compare?

The next step is for the teacher to record the ideas on the chalkboard as each group reports. As I record the items, I ask questions that encourage students to expand on what they mean. This often introduces new ideas, facts or concepts to others in the class. In fact, it's a method of subtly introducing material to students who don't know it. I try to be interested in and encouraging about every prediction, saying things like, "So, nocturnal means only coming out at night. Oh good, that's really interesting." Furthermore, I never correct erroneous information—this will happen naturally during the next stage of the exercise.

When all the brainstormed ideas have been recorded, students are ready to read the selected passage. As they do, they check off the items they correctly predicted and note things they didn't know or expect. Recording these in a column beside the predictions seems to help readers compare the items they expected with those they didn't.

I've asked many different groups of adult readers in many parts of North America to read passages about scorpions from newspapers, science textbooks and general information texts.

The following are some of the items they've identified as things they didn't expect to read or didn't know:

— scorpions have twelve eyes
— they can't kill other scorpions with their venom
— there are more than 1,000 species of scorpions
— they look like eight-legged spiders
— the smallest ones are the most dangerous
— seven kinds have fatal stings
— the tail has a hollow needle-like stinger
— the venom affects nerves
— they hunt only at night
— they hang onto the undersides of things
— they can live to be twenty-five years old
— they eat insects, snakes, lizards and other scorpions
— the young hang onto mother's back
— antivenom helps save people from death
— they have been around for 350 million years

After the reading—and after the groups have discussed their brainstormed predictions—I read each item from the chalkboard list, saying, for example, "It says that scorpions sting with their tails curved over their head. Is this right?"

When predictions are confirmed, I place a + next to the item. An X marks incorrect items, though I'm careful not to make negative comments about these. A question mark indicates predictions that were neither confirmed nor disconfirmed. Research can reveal more information about these items.

Thus, an excerpt from the left-hand column of the pre-reading list might end up looking like this:

+ scorpions sting with their curved tails over their head
? black scorpions are an evil omen (Hong Kong)
? powdered small brown scorpions are an aphrodisiac
+ scorpions live under rocks
+ they scurry
? they are dropped into the shirts of unsuspecting tourists in Mexico
X they are insects

Brainstorming before reading is an interesting activity that generates a great deal of enthusiasm and learning. It's also an instructive exercise for teachers, a form of needs assessment that tells us whether further instruction is necessary. In the case of the scorpion exercise, for example, many individuals identify scorpions as insects, obviously an area that requires further instruction. The exercise also identifies areas that particular students have great knowledge of and interest in.

This activity also gives readers a very personal reason for reading. As the reading progresses, it's interesting to note the conversation that goes on. Students say things like, "You were right," and "I didn't know that," indicating that they are becoming active, interested readers.

Pre-reading brainstorming provides students with a kind of reading guide because they look for items they predicted. In addition, items that were not expected stand out, thus becoming more memorable.

Once the activity is over, teachers must judge where and how to continue the learning experience. A teacher may decide, for example, that students have learned enough, making further study unnecessary. Some students, however, may have become so fascinated that they want to learn more.

I once introduced this exercise to students in a secondary school ESL classroom. A week later, I received a call from the regular teacher saying that one student had become so enthralled by scorpions that he'd purchased one for a pet and brought it to school. Yes, it lived in a cage and ate crickets mercilessly dropped into the cage by the owner. The teacher reported that this rather large brown creature was likely the best-fed scorpion in the world and had the potential to become the fattest. On other occasions, students have sent me interesting articles about scorpions from around the world.

The "scorpion" procedure may be effectively extended to include making a pre-reading graphic, such as a semantic web, focusing on the material students brainstormed or on the vocabulary we, as teachers, identify as important or basic to the passage.

A semantic web is a kind of visual representation of knowledge. In an article in *Reading Research Quarterly*, Bernie Armbruster, Thomas Anderson and Joyce Ostertag indicate that creating semantic webs or maps has positive effects on learning both vocabulary and content from text.

After brainstorming the list of information about scorpions and before inviting students to read the article, I might have asked them to construct a web based on their predictions. The following vocabulary list is from an article on crustaceans. See if you can organize the words into a web.

Abdomen	Animals	Antenna	Barnacles
Branchiopods	Carapace	Chela	Cirripedes
Copepods	Crabs	Crayfish	Crustaceans
Cuticle	Exoskeleton	Fish-lice	Head
Insects	Larva	Life cycle	Lobsters
Malacostracans	Nauplius	Oceans	Ostracods
Parasitic	Plankton	Pleopods	Prawns
Regeneration	Shrimp	Slaters	Thorax
Trunk	Wood lice		

This task is actually easier than it seems. Even if you're no expert on crustaceans, you probably know enough to create a web, especially if you can include an "I don't know" category.

New reading tasks should not contain material that is totally unknown; if students can make absolutely no sense of the material, then it's too difficult. Jean Piaget suggested that a moderate degree of novelty in learning tasks is appropriate— students should know enough about the new material for it to make sense within the context of what they already know.

The following web was created by a group of twelve- and thirteen-year-olds from the "crustaceans" vocabulary list:

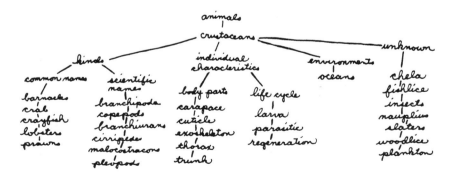

What logic produced this web? First, the students decided that crustaceans are animals—and placed "animals" at the top of the web. Because they were told only that the passage would be about crustaceans, their next category was "crustaceans." They didn't have a copy of the passage and couldn't check titles and subtitles to see how the author had divided the material, so they started from the bottom to see if there were some obvious groupings into which they could organize the remaining words.

Because the list of words was so long, the students wrote each word on a card and sorted through them, grouping those that made sense. This exercise helped them come up with the next level of categories—kinds, individual characteristics, environment and unknown. They then decided that there are common and scientific names for crustaceans, so they divided the kinds into these two groups. The scientific names were selected because they "sounded like" scientific names.

This activity invited students to apply logic to a list of vocabulary before they read the passage. In effect, it required them to use their background knowledge to make sense out of the list. The pre-reading web they produced maps out roughly a great deal of the information presented in the text.

This web can then be used to generate sentences like the following that become the basis for questions that form a kind of study guide:

— Crustaceans are animals.
— Barnacle is a common name for a kind of crustacean.
— Branchiopod is a scientific name for a kind of crustacean.
— The carapace, cuticle, exoskeleton, thorax and trunk are individual parts of crustaceans.

It may be necessary to help students form sentences by showing them that the process involves working up the structure of a web, from specific to general categories.

Each of the sentences can then be used to form questions like the following:

— Are crustaceans animals?
— Are the terms branchiopods, copepods, branchiurans, cirripedes, malacostracans and pleopods the scientific names of crustaceans? Unknown items can also be turned into questions (e.g., "What does chela mean?").

The questions generated this way help guide students' reading of the passage.

You may be convinced that the students in your class are incapable of doing something like this. And they may be! What they need, of course, is your careful guidance, your expert teaching.

Select a passage, perhaps one from a science book. Make a list of the vocabulary you think is important, put it on an overhead transparency and write individual words on cards. Talk about how the list might be organized into categories. Ask for possible categories. Invite a group of students to sort the word cards into categories. Practice generating sentences and questions. Finally, write out the questions produced by the exercise. This is the study guide. For the passage about crustaceans, it might look like this:

1. Crustaceans are animals. __ Yes __No

   _____

2. The carapace is the body part of a crustacean. __Yes __No

   _____

3. Barnacles are branchiopods. __Yes __No

   _____

4. Chela is a crustacean. __Yes __No

   _____

5. Insects are crustaceans. __Yes __No

   _____

Summary

Things I learned from reading this passage that I didn't know or expect to find out are:

   _____

   _____

Display the passage on an overhead transparency, read it together and answer the questions as the information becomes available. If "no" is the answer to a question, write the correct answer in the space below. As the passage is read and questions are answered, information not covered in the study guide will be discovered. This can be recorded at the bottom. Often, this section of the guide is the most rewarding for students because they learn material they hadn't anticipated.

The final step can be to rearrange the pre-reading web into a post-reading web. This is a kind of final comprehension exercise that indicates students' final understanding of the passage. The post-reading web produced by the same group of twelve- and thirteen-year-olds looked like this:

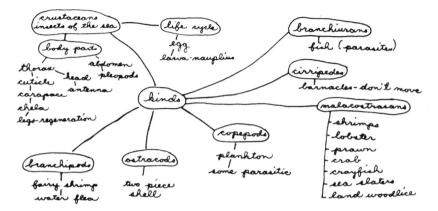

When I asked the group why they had changed their web, their explanation demonstrated clearly that they had comprehended the material and understood the relationships described in the passage. Indeed, even when used with adults, this activity clearly improves comprehension of material that is complex and densely written, especially when it is filled with specialized vocabulary.

Summary

Even experts sometimes find content or academic text difficult to read because the writing is often complex and obscure. A teacher's first task is to determine what students must and should learn. An unthinking reliance on curriculum guides to make educational decisons surrenders the teacher's most important role to the author(s) of these guides, who are often anonymous, known only as "them" or "they."

Deciding what to teach is not always easy because it requires the time, and in many cases, the courage to face the political consequences of determining what students' education should be. When teachers opt to take charge and make their own educational decisions, they also empower students to play an active role in their own learning.

Content reading is a serious business. This chapter presented strategies that incorporate students' abilities to make predictions about content or academic texts, procedures that develop student-generated background information to guide the reading process. The strategies are based on the notion that good readers are active predictors who apply their background knowledge to text in creative ways. In many respects, content-subject teachers are responsible for equipping students with reading skills that will help them survive in our technological society. While this chapter has focused on reading for information, the next will focus on critical reading, equipping students to make judgments about the texts they read.

THE BEST WIDGETS
IN THE WORLD

In the beginning, there was the word. Because they believe that the printed word is the truth, some readers have blind faith in printed texts. Yet authors present material that may vary from outright falsehood to opinion, to considered opinion, to truth. Because readers must be critical of the material they read, teachers must equip students with the skills they need to be critical readers. Asking students to read material simply to answer questions on a quiz, worksheet or exam isn't enough. They need to know how to ignore systematically some material, how to search systematically for other material, and how to judge whether what they read is true. This chapter focuses on the skills students need to become critical readers.

Purpose of Reading and Reading Rate

Mature readers change their reading rates depending upon their purposes for reading and, of course, the "difficulty" of the material. Reading an entertaining story while sitting in front of a warm fireplace is considerably different from reading a treatise on realist epistemology in preparation for a final exam. Experienced readers slow down when the material is difficult and speed up when they are skimming or scanning.

SKIMMING

Skimming is faster than general reading. Its purpose is to discover general information from a text. It's a valuable skill, one to be used when assessing information sources, discovering main ideas and themes, and assessing whether material should be read more thoroughly. Think about what happens in book stores. We flip through books to find out if they contain interesting material. When we find something that catches our attention, we stop, slow down and savor it.

How do students determine whether a particular book meets their needs before they buy it? How do they find out if a book contains the information needed for a particular project or class? Skimming is the answer.

The following are signposts to look for while skimming:

— The title.
— Descriptive information provided by the publisher.
— The foreword, preface or introduction.
— The table of contents (especially the chapter titles).
— Information highlighted in some way (e.g., text presented in boxes).

Many students, even at university, are uncomfortable with skimming because they're convinced their task is to read and comprehend every word in a text. And, to be truthful, there are times when every word *may* be important—when reading a recipe, for example.

However, the ability to skim is also important. If students need help to learn it, select a passage they haven't seen before and give them a time limit, such as fifteen seconds, and a purpose for reading like, "Read to find out what this passage is about." After a few practice sessions with different passages, students will become much better at skimming.

After they've skimmed the passage, ask them to record as many items as they can. They might do this in groups. Begin with short passages and progress to whole books. Challenge them to discover the major contents of a book within two minutes. It's amazing how much they come up with if they've been taught to identify important signposts, a topic covered in the section titled "Taking Off the Training Wheels."

SCANNING

If students wish to discover the most important grain crop in Kansas, they don't need to read an entire chapter word by word. Instead, they can scan to find the information.

Newspapers are excellent sources of cheap scanning material. Very often, community newspapers will provide classrooms with free, though dated, copies on a regular basis.

To begin, transfer an article to an overhead transparency and give students a purpose for reading it. If the article is about the political situation in Ethiopia, for example, the teacher might say, "Read this paragraph to find out what the new government of Ethiopia is."

Students can raise their hands as soon as they know the answer or they can be asked to write their answers independently after seeing the article for about twenty seconds. It doesn't take long for them to learn to scan. Skimming and scanning provide a foundation for teaching other vital content reading strategies.

EVALUATING EDITORIAL FEATURES

Through experience, most adult readers have come to understand that because something is in print doesn't necessarily mean it's true. Nevertheless, the huge sales of tabloid newspapers at the checkout counter of every large supermarket are eloquent testimony to the human faith in the printed word.

Once readers have understood a text, it's critical that they be able to make judgments about the author's message. Is the content fact or opinion? Is it propaganda? Are the author's arguments logical and supported? Is the material valuable? Even primary students must learn that they need to make judgments about text.

Teaching students to recognize some of the vocabulary associated with opinion and propaganda begins to make them aware that they can distinguish fact from opinion in print. Some words that may signal that an opinion is being given are "should," "may," "perhaps," "would," "could," "possible," "possibly," "if," "might," "think," "suggest," "believe," "probably," "apparently," "likely," "allegedly," and so on.

Consider these statements, for example:

— The president believes free trade is good for America.
— The rains apparently washed out the bridge.
— Research suggests that poor readers are anxious readers.

These words are not always present, however. For example, what features of a sentence such as, "Kline's cars are the best in the world," determine that it is an opinion rather than a fact? Is there something about the surface structure of sentences that helps readers make initial judgments about their truth? Consider the following:

— About 25,000 people die of lung cancer every year in the United States.
— Pollution is possibly the most dangerous health hazard in the world.
— Happiness is the most important element in life.
— Democracy is better than any other form of government.
— A hug every morning is good for you.

The first sentence is verifiable because readers can check it out. If it turned out to be untrue, readers understand that it is a mistake or a fabrication, not an expression of opinion. The second sentence, on the other hand, is clearly an opinion signaled by the word "possibly." What about the other statements? What are the features that tell proficient readers that these are opinions rather than facts?

After considering a series of statements like this, one nine-year-old told me, "You have to watch out for good, better and best sentences." He also suggested that the value of the opinion depends upon the credibility of the person who expresses it, indicating that he was making a critical judgment about the speaker's—or writer's—expertise in making an evaluation. This boy had become a critical reader.

Let's consider an issue; in this case, free trade. Read the following passage and mark the items you suspect are opinion rather than fact.

Free Trade
by
Sir Tackson Yew

The world has become a global village, one in which geopolitical boundaries have no more meaning than the streets that divide a city. International trade provides the bananas eaten in Fairbanks, Alaska, in December, the Toyotas driven in Saudi Arabia, the gasoline used in cars in Osaka, Japan, the rubber gloves, the stainless-steel prosthetics, the antibiotics and the x-ray equipment used in operations in Mexico City to replace broken hips, the chopsticks and rice on dinner tables in Singapore, the cigarettes smoked in Argentina, and the computer programs used in a million computers around the world.

The world has become a large market. Only its petty leaders and repressive governments retard the pace of trade and make it difficult for the world to become a truly open, single market where free trade flourishes. This is a pity because it slows economic development and results in higher prices as governments try to protect non-competitive businesses. Free trade encourages development and results in more prosperity for more people. Free trade is the wave of the future.

Distinguishing fact from opinion in this passage may not be as easy as it seems. Let's look at some of the statements in isolation:

— International trade provides the bananas eaten in Fairbanks, Alaska, in December, the Toyotas driven in Saudi Arabia, the gasoline used in cars in Osaka, Japan, the rubber gloves, the stainless-steel prosthetics, the antibiotics, and the x-ray equipment used in operations in Mexico City to replace broken hips, the chopsticks and rice on dinner tables in Singapore, the cigarettes smoked in Argentina, and the computer programs used in a million computers around the world.
— ...its (the world's) petty leaders and repressive governments retard the pace of trade and make it difficult for the world to become a truly open, single market ....
— Free trade encourages development and results in more prosperity for more people.

Many of these statements appear to be facts, items based on knowledge rather than opinion—but are they really? How would a reader go about finding out whether particular statements are true? It's worth keeping in mind, too, that "facts" change, often very quickly. For instance, a few years ago I learned the annual average tonnage of bananas produced by Brazil, knowledge that is now outdated. How can we teach students to judge? In the case of the article on free trade, judging is not easy because many of the signal words mentioned earlier are missing. Our initial judgment about the validity of the statements may be based on a different kind of information—our assessment of the expertise of the author or a belief that our teacher would provide us only with material that is true and valid.

By the way, this is why it's so important for us to consider carefully what we teach. Students tend to believe that what we teach is true, important and worth knowing. We make no judgment as important as this.

Opinion varies in "weight." A Nobel prize-winner's opinion on economics—if the award was for economics—may be more valid than the local bartender's. However, opinion can be dangerous if believed without reservation, evaluation and thought. Try the following exercise:

Who Says?

The following opinions are stated by various people. Whose do you trust? Rate each on the following scale:

1— Trust Completely
2— Trust
3— Neither Trust nor Distrust
4— Distrust
5— Distrust Completely

The President of the United States says that income taxes need to be increased.
_____ (Rating)

Mrs. Adams, president of the school board, says that teachers' salaries are too high.
_____ (Rating)

It was the consensus of the International Panel on AIDS meeting in San Francisco that infections will continue to rise around the world in the '90s, particularly in third-world countries.
_____ (Rating)

Older students quickly become critical readers after completing a few exercises like this. Newspapers can provide a host of statements students can be asked to judge. For example, I drew the following items from the *Vancouver Sun*, my morning newspaper:

— A major Canadian study of mammography has found no apparent benefit from routine breast screening for women under 50, says the deputy director of the study.
— Russian leaders appear to be on a collision course over whether a multi-billion-dollar blueprint for a Western economic backup of Russian reforms is a grand bargain or a grand illusion.
— The Free Trade Agreement with the United States is an easy target for its opponents because its costs, in terms of lost jobs and business, are much more visible than its benefits in encouraging foreign investment and opening American markets to Canadian products.

These statements carry some authority because they are from a newspaper. Still, we must make judgments about opinion. Discussing students' reasons for making particular judgments enables teachers to assess their reasoning and thinking. Often, judgments are based on biases, prejudices learned through listening to others, especially adults.

Readers must be equipped to judge what is true, what is real knowledge and what is opinion. In fact, it cannot be said that we know something unless we have the appropriate justification for our knowledge. In *Conditions of Knowledge*, Israel Scheffler stated, "In educative contexts, in particular, our purpose is to develop the child's autonomous appraisals of his own beliefs, by standards of evidence we ourselves hold appropriate." Readers must have good reason to believe that something is true. "My teacher told me it's right" is a good reason only for very small children.

The successful independent reader, then, is able to:

— Skim a book or article to discover whether it contains needed information or material.
— Scan a book or article to find particular items of information or material.
— Identify signal words that suggest material may be opinion rather than fact.
— Assess the "weight" of a particular author's opinion.
— Judge whether there is good reason or a good case to indicate that the material is fact rather than opinion.
— Judge the relative merit of an opinion by assessing the author's expertise.

Returning to the article on free trade that appeared earlier in this chapter, let's examine how these skills can be applied. The following statement about the North American Free Trade Agreement (NAFTA) can be presented to students both before and after reading the article:

North American free trade is good for the United States, Canada and Mexico.

Before Reading

Agree   Disagree

After Reading

Agree   Disagree

If you were asked to write a series of statements explaining why you do or don't support the agreement, you would likely be able to list several pros and cons. I encouraged students to try to produce as many statements on both sides of the issue as possible. After they were noted and discussed in groups, they were reported orally to the class and written on the chalkboard. Again, the teacher questions students' statements, explores their reasoning, and reviews the material they have produced. Here's a list of some of the pros and cons produced by one group of seventeen- and eighteen-year-olds.

Agree

— It's good for business so it will be good for the people of all three countries.
— It lets good Canadian businesses have a bigger market in the United States and Mexico and makes less efficient businesses improve or go out of business.
— It will give Canadian consumers a chance to buy cheaper products from the United States and Mexico.

Disagree

— Canada is too small to compete with the United States and Mexico.
— The United States will demand to get Canada's natural resources and Mexico's labor force.
— It will make Canadians and Americans have a lower standard of living because they will have to compete with Mexican businesses that pay below minimum

wages and no social benefits and do not have to pay for environmental protection efforts. Canada and the United States will have higher unemployment.
— Thousands of Canadian and American jobs and companies will move to Mexico where the operating expenses are lower. This will result in continued economic recession and loss of jobs in the United States and Mexico.
— Canada will become just another one of the states and will lose all its national and international status and prestige, while the United States will become a service-based economy that will not produce durable goods.

As before, it's possible to help guide students' reading by restating the statements as questions. The following are examples of questions about North American free trade that appeared on a self-generated study guide:

1. Will NAFTA be good for business?
2. Will NAFTA be good for Canadians? For Americans? For Mexicans?
3. Will NAFTA give good businesses bigger markets?
4. Will NAFTA make less efficient businesses improve or go out of business?
5. Will NAFTA give consumers a chance to buy cheaper products?
6. Will NAFTA lower prices of imported goods?
7. Is Canada too small to compete with the United States? Is Canada too small to compete with Mexico?
8. Will Canadian and American businesses move to Mexico?
9. Will pollution increase because of industry moving to Mexico where there are fewer environmental protection laws?

A group-generated study guide, consisting of questions students formulate themselves, helps improve their comprehension of text. Variety and a little friendly competition may be introduced to this activity by asking groups to focus strictly on positive or negative statements. This compels the groups to brainstorm ideas in a particular direction, encouraging students to explore an issue—and defend ideas—from a point of view that may not necessarily be their own. Here's how a typical lesson might proceed:

— The teacher states an issue such as, "Women should be allowed to enter combat as members of the armed forces."
— The class is divided into groups, perhaps using cooperative grouping.
— The teacher randomly assigns "pro" or "con" groups. This can be done by having two groups at a time call heads or tails as a coin is tossed.
— The groups are given ten or fifteen minutes to compile a list of statements supporting or refuting the statement.
— The chalkboard is divided in half and points made by the "pro" side are written and discussed first. As in the previous activities, the teacher encourages discussion by assuming the role of naive reporter. The "con" statements are then added.
— Students are given the passage to read as groups to find support for their statements.
— After twenty-or-so minutes, the groups are called together and attention is focused on the items written on the chalkboard. Groups are asked to quote statements or information from the reading to support their earlier points. Because this can be a volatile period, the teacher must maintain good control.
— New ideas may come up during this discussion. Some items may remain contentious or unanswered even after reading the passage. As in previous activities, this calls for further research.

During this activity, students question authors' opinions and their qualifications to hold them, the degree to which the text represents fact or opinion, the language of the text and the scope of the text. In essence, it helps them become critical readers—the goal of every reading program.

But Can They Read It Independently?

The group activities discussed so far help produce active critical readers. They also help many students become independent critical readers without much more instruction. However, some students may need further individual help. Indeed, teachers may decide to involve all students in the following activities designed to help readers form a plan or interactive strategy for independently comprehending and learning from academic material.

Content texts are different from elementary reading texts in ways that were pointed out at the beginning of this chapter. The following list, which is far from comprehensive, reveals that a surprising number of special skills are needed to read content texts independently.

— Recognize the significance of the content.
— Recognize important details.
— Find the main idea of a paragraph.
— Find the main idea of sections of discourse.
— Differentiate fact from opinion.
— Locate topic sentences.
— Locate answers to specific questions.
— Make inferences about content.
— Critically evaluate content.
— Realize an author's purpose.
— Determine the accuracy of information.
— Use a table of contents.
— Use an index.
— Use appendixes.
— Read and interpret tables, charts and graphs.
— Read and interpret maps, diagrams and illustrative material.
— Read and interpret formulas.
— Read and understand written problems.
— Read and understand argument.
— Adjust reading rate relative to purpose for reading.
— Adjust reading rate relative to difficulty of material.
— Scan for specific information.
— Skim for important ideas.
— Learn new material from text.

Elementary teachers need to assess students' content reading abilities—their strengths and weaknesses—in order to decide who may need more explicit instruction. A content reading inventory like that described in the section of this chapter titled "How to Tell if Students Have Content Reading Problems" helps do this.

The following activities focus on the standard features of content material, those that often cause students difficulty. These features are associated with "content structure." Indeed, they represent a kind of general background knowledge. An ability to use these features as "signposts" of content structure helps students comprehend and learn from text, both in standard academic texts and technical material.

Textbook authors attempt to present material they believe students should learn in coherent, organized ways. Students who are familiar with the pattern of the underlying discourse structures used in particular texts are more likely to comprehend the material they are reading. These structures vary from subject to subject in fairly systematic ways.

Textbooks in subjects such as geography, history, social studies, economics, sociology and psychology often contain expository writing and specialized vocabulary. Mathematics textbooks are filled with symbols, diagrams and mathematical formulas in addition to text that is often loaded with difficult vocabulary and presented in the form of intense analytical discourse. Like mathematics texts, science texts also contain specialized, difficult vocabulary and complex, analytical expository prose, as well as charts, graphs, diagrams and mathematical equations. They often require students to analyze data and predict outcomes.

Courses in the humanities require students to read different kinds of texts altogether. English literature courses, for example, require students to read narrative texts. They may be asked to consider the qualities of the prose, analyze characters' motivations, judge events, draw inferences and interpret styles of writing. In other areas of the humanities, they may be asked to interpret moods and feelings or consider the importance of events or trends in, for example, fashion or art.

Unfortunately, text structures don't always fall neatly into these categories. Like the concept of story grammar discussed previously, the characteristics described here are generalizations that may not apply consistently.

This leaves teachers with two alternatives: teach strategies that are so general that they provide comprehension assistance regardless of the specific text structures; or take complete control of students' comprehension and produce study guides to help them read specific passages.

Study guides highlight the important points contained in a text, points selected by the teacher. While they do help students comprehend difficult text, they also place responsibility for this comprehension in the teacher's hands. Nevertheless, they can be used as transitional aids to help students develop independent content reading strategies. A typical teacher-prepared study guide might contain material like this:

1. Look at the title of the chapter on page 165. What kind of subjects do you think will be covered in this chapter?
2. Look at the subtitle on page 178. It says, "Hermeneutics and the Teaching of Language Arts." What is hermeneutics?

It's important to remember that, if used too often, study guides become no more meaningful than worksheets. There is a risk that readers will ignore information not mentioned in the study guide, scanning the text to find only the information the teacher has identified as important. We must teach students to develop their own study guides, much like the group-generated guides discussed earlier. If students can do this, have been taught to skim and scan and can distinguish fact from opinion, they're well-equipped to read text independently. However, they may need training in one final content reading skill—using graphic aids.

Ideally, readers should be able to determine what information is available in a graphic. For our purposes, it's enough for them to be able to look at a graphic and construct a question based on the information it contains. The ability to formulate these questions helps readers understand their texts more completely. They often find it easier to formulate questions based on charts, tables and so on if they have created their own graphic aids. To provide this experience, invite them to create graphics to represent classroom data like the following:

— The month of birth of students in the class.
— The month of birth of the boys—and girls—in the class.
— The number of students who prefer pencils to pens.
— The number of boys—and girls—who prefer pencils to pens.
— The number of boys—and girls—who prefer pencils to pens according to their month of birth.

Encourage students to label their graphics carefully, as they are in any good textbook. Then, use one of their graphics to help them generate a series of questions based on the relationships shown in the graphic. The following graphic might have been created by students asked to complete the preceding exercise:

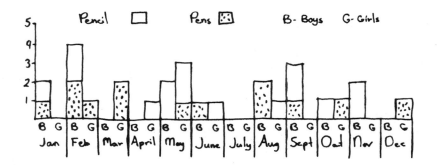

After creating the graphic, students might come up with questions like the following:

— Are pencils or pens more popular?
— If you were born in February, are you more likely to prefer a pencil or pen?
— On average, who prefers to use pencils—girls or boys?

SQ3R

The strategies discussed so far in this chapter are designed to prepare students to read content material independently. SQ3R, a strategy set out by Frances Robinson in *Effective Study*, is designed to increase students' retention of content material. While it's certainly an old standby and somewhat rigid, it, nevertheless, effectively incorporates many of the comprehension strategies discussed in this chapter and helps students develop their own study guides.

SQ3R stands for survey, question, read, recite and review.

Survey: Once the reading material is selected, students are invited to survey it, beginning with the title. If there is a chapter outline, it is surveyed to discover the topics or ideas covered. If there is no outline, the table of contents can often be used for the same purpose. Students read the titles and subtitles found in the chapter, captions and titles associated with the graphic aids, summaries, and questions posed by the author. They also look for special vocabulary, which is often highlighted in content texts. If the meanings of the words are unknown, a trip to the glossary or a dictionary is essential.

Question: To guide their comprehension, students formulate and record questions involving all titles, subtitles, summaries and graphic aids. "What is the significance of the chart on page 3?" and "Why does the author condemn some genetic research?" are examples of questions they may come up with.

Read: Students read the chapter carefully to find the answers to their questions, taking notes as they go. In many cases, they will find that some of their questions were slightly off base. This step provides them with an opportunity to reformulate and answer the questions.

Recite: Textbook chapters are usually divided into sections. At the end of each section, readers stop to recite the answer— either orally or in writing—to the questions developed for the section—without looking back at the text.

Review: After students have finished reading the chapter, they review their questions and answers. Like the "recite" step, this review is often more effective when done a section at a time.

As they become more proficient content readers, most students will begin to streamline the SQ3R procedure. Some readers, however, are unable to sustain the discipline required to apply SQ3R consistently. Nevertheless, they should be encouraged to try, because there are very positive benefits.

For many students, the most difficult aspect of SQ3R is constructing the questions. To overcome this difficulty, I cut and laminate a one-inch strip of paper that aligns to the text of each page of the selected reading. The strip points out the items students should turn into questions. When the reading involves a long chapter, I punch holes in the tops of the strips and hold them together with a shower ring.

BUT IS THIS AN INTEGRATED APPROACH TO READING AND WRITING?

SQ3R has been around a long time, is fairly teacher-directed, and doesn't encourage students to interact with content text independently or to become proficient content readers in a natural or holistic way. This may be true. However, academic or content text isn't necessarily natural, doesn't necessarily contain natural language, and is often filled with difficult concepts and ideas and incredibly complex writing structures.

SQ3R certainly isn't for everyone. It's for students who have difficulty reading content text even after participating in the interactive group activities discussed previously. It focuses students' attention on textual features that represent signposts to the content of textbooks. If you find SQ3R too mechanistic and teacher-imposed, creating content webs may be an alternative.

Content Webs

Content webs are similar to the pre-reading webs described in the previous chapter. When creating them, however, students have the text at hand. The following procedure works well:

— Use section titles, if available, to develop major categories for the web.
— If there are no titles, skim the passage to find a statement of a main idea or subject.
— Skim the text to find unknown or unusual vocabulary and place the words in the web. Formulate a question using this vocabulary.
— Identify, if possible, an introductory sentence or paragraph that communicates the main idea(s) to be developed or a final paragraph or sentence that summarizes the main idea of the section or chapter.
— Assess any graphic material, formulate a question to be answered, and record vocabulary associated with the graphic that might help understand it.
— Read the passage carefully, answer the questions formulated earlier, and define new or unknown terms.
— Reformulate the web after reading, taking into account new information that has been learned.

Content webbing is less rigorous for students and less structured than SQ3R. While students find it fairly easy, it effectively increases their comprehension of text and works well with many different kinds of content material. It can, of course, be adapted in a variety of ways to match students' needs.

Finding Out If Students Have Content Reading Problems

This chapter has contained strategies to help students improve their comprehension and retention of content material. By and large, the strategies presented have been holistic, focusing on the process of learning new material. Nevertheless, it's obvious that content reading requires certain skills that are, in many cases, specific and discrete. Knowing how to use a table of contents, for instance, is an extremely important skill that some students don't learn without direct instruction.

Before assigning texts for reading, teachers should know, in general terms, whether students can read and comprehend the material. We should also be aware that specific students may need help to strengthen certain content reading skills.

To assess the appropriateness of the match between readers and content texts and to measure students' content reading strengths and weaknesses, teachers can conduct an overall comprehension assessment and a content-specific inventory.

THE CLOZE PROCEDURE

Cloze exercises can help measure general comprehension and readability and match students with the appropriate texts. This particular version of cloze involves deleting words systematically from a passage and asking students to draw on their knowledge of syntax and semantics to fill in the blanks.

To prepare a series of cloze passages, follow these steps:

— Select a passage of about 250 running words from the middle of a text that students haven't read before but are expected to read.
— Retype the passage, double- or triple-spaced, leaving the title and the first and last sentences intact.
— Beginning with the second sentence, delete every fifth word, including contractions, hyphenations, and numerals, such as 1999.
— In place of each deleted word, type a horizontal line. It's important that the lines be equal in length.

— Invite students to fill in the blanks—without referring to the original text. It may be necessary to select passages from texts at several reading levels before achieving the best student-text match.
— Accepting as correct only items that are *exactly* the same as the original.
— Although scoring citeria vary, most educators appear to use the Bormuth criteria as follows:

Independent Level	Instructional Level	Frustration Level
50% +	38-49%	37% -

Students operating at the independent level will comprehend the text with no help from the teacher. At the instructional level, which is ideal, they will need help from the teacher. If they're at the frustration level, however, no amount of help will do because the text is simply too difficult.

When ESL students are involved, I raise the criteria somewhat to account for the content vocabulary and knowledge. In fact, even when dealing with native English speakers, I find that a score of 50 to 69 per cent indicates that students are at the instructional level.

IT COULD BE A CLOZE CALL

Some authorities believe that this version of cloze does not precisely predict whether students will comprehend a particular text. In fact, a miscue analysis, including comprehension questions, is a better measure. Unfortunately, this procedure is time-consuming because teachers must deal with students individually, then analyze the reading performance of each.

Here are several pros and cons related to the use of cloze:

— Cloze tests are easy to produce and score.
— Cloze scores should be considered general indicators, rather than a precise measurement of reading comprehension.
— Cloze tests are frustrating for students.
— Cloze scores vary a great deal in their reliability.

Cloze assessments provide a general, though sometimes inaccurate, measure of comprehension. We must decide whether having no information about students' comprehension is better than having some information, even though it may not be highly reliable. If teachers decide not to include cloze in their assessment repertoire, the content reading inventory described next still provides valuable information about how well students can understand and use the content features of the text.

CONTENT READING INVENTORY

Once students' ability to comprehend their content texts is clear, it's a good idea to find out whether they understand the special features of content material, some of which were noted earlier in this chapter. This requires construction of a content inventory.

The most important goal of a content inventory is to find out whether students possess the skills required to read a particular text. Many texts, for instance, include time-line maps. If students don't know how to read these, they won't understand an important part of the text.

The first step is to assess carefully the particular text students are being asked to read to decide which skills are required. For example, are students required to read and learn from graphs? Are they expected to be able to use a glossary? We must judge what the important content features are.

Leaf through the text tallying features on a table like the one on the following page. It reveals the skills required to read the text. Once this is done, the next task is to construct an assessment to measure students' needs and abilities with reference to it. Earlier, I noted some of the differences in style that occur between subject areas. These must also be considered.

As many questions as possible should be generated without making the assessment exhaustive—about twenty are usually adequate. If the text focuses on main idea, the assessment should include many questions about main idea (e.g., Read the paragraph about the westward expansion. What is the main idea of the passage?).

Explain the goal of the inventory, stressing that it isn't a test in the usual sense because students won't receive a grade. Then, invite them to read the selected text. After they finish, ask them to answer the questions by referring to the text—or without referring to the text iIf absolute recall is expected.

This is an informal test and shouldn't be used to establish grades. The following scoring guidelines were suggested by Marty Ruddell:

— 90 per cent and higher—student is able to use the textual features independently.
— 65-90 per cent—student needs instruction in using the textual features.
— 65 per cent and lower—if a student's cloze score is also at the instructional or frustration level, the text may be beyond his or her capacity to read and comprehend.

Based on the content inventory, teachers can create an assessment table like the following, adapted from *ESL Literacy Instruction*. The identified content skills are listed across the top. The chart identifies students with similar strengths and weaknesses and can be used both to plan instruction and group students for instruction.

Content Features Assessment Record

Name	1*	2	3	4	5	6	7	8
Philip								
Greg								
Susanne								
Jamal								

* 1. Table of contents 2. Glossary 3. Find main idea 4. Read maps 5. Follow directions 6. Follow sequence of cause-and-effect statements 7. Read and interpret pie charts and bar graphs 8. Read and understand "flow" maps

Summary

This chapter has presented strategies to help students become critical readers by equipping them to make judgments about the validity and reliability of the information in texts. It has also presented an assessment procedure to judge the content reading skills students possess or need to learn. The following chapters describe assessment procedures and the classroom integration of learning programs.

. . . .

KEEPING THE WAREHOUSE

IN ORDER

There is probably no worse time to hold teaching workshops than after school. So when Sylvia McKinnon and I found ourselves representing our school at a late-afternoon workshop on individualization one day, we were tired and less than enthusiastic. Our task was to absorb the information, then return to our school to help the other teachers individualize instruction, a stated goal of our superintendent. Both of us were veterans of workshops and conferences, used to hearing ideas that sounded wonderful until the time came to implement them in our classrooms—classrooms that were inconsiderately filled with living, squirming, impatient children. Something magical often happens in the typical classroom— something that makes the best-sounding strategies impractical, impossible to implement and frustrating to maintain.

This time, however, things seemed different. Despite our fatigue, we were inspired by the presentations and buoyed by the enthusiasm of the instructors, representatives of an educational publishing firm. It didn't occur to us to question their motives or their focus on the firm's product as the primary tool of the individualized program they described.

In fact, my first hesitation didn't surface until about two weeks later. At 7:30 one morning, I sat in my empty classroom, facing the individualized reading program and all its components. It was time to implement it. How to begin?

The events are still etched in my memory. First, I had to give everyone a pre-test to determine entry levels. Sounded easy enough—but neither I nor the program's authors had anticipated the false fire alarm, the two kids who stayed home sick, the principal summoning a problem student to the office, the two students who were withdrawn for special testing, the bilingual support teacher's request for a conference with two Tagalog-speaking students, the film shown by one of my open-area pod partners and the music lesson of another, a room-mother arriving to ask for volunteers for the cake sale, and the five crossing-guard members who left for a meeting with the supervising police officer. Of course, none of this was particularly unusual for the first half-hour of class.

I managed, somehow, to get most of the students tested. That night, as I corrected math worksheets, the weekend writing homework and a social studies test, I also pondered the students' reading pre-test scores and began to plan the procedures for matching them with the reading materials.

By the next morning, I had neatly filled in the pages of the loose-leaf binder that formed the core of the management system and printed the students' names in an appropriate student response booklet, indicating the color-code of their starting levels in my teacher's record. At the beginning of class, I patiently demonstrated the system according to the model lesson the publisher had conveniently provided.

Finally, we were ready to begin. Each student had been thoroughly prepared. The program included a series of stories, organized on color-coded cards and stored in a box. The colors represented different achievement levels, but students weren't supposed to know that. Unfortunately, the kit didn't contain enough copies of each story to get all the students started at the appropriate level at the same time. In fact, the way things worked out, only about half the class could start at once. So I tried to keep the other half occupied drawing pictures, talking about reading, passing the time productively, doing any kind of busy work I could find.

As one student finished a card, I collected the material and gave it to someone else who needed it. After three days of this, each student was finally matched with the correct material. My job was to manage their learning, hold individual conferences with them, correct the end-of-section tests, make certain they kept the kit in good order, and keep records of their progress, including detailed minutes of each conference.

By about the end of the second week, I realized the new program wasn't working very well—for me or the students. Here are some of the problems I found:

— The individual conferences took a great deal of time. In fact, I could see each student only about once a week. Sometimes I completely missed students who were sick or involved in another school activity or because I was busy with other students and simply ran out of time.
— Story cards got lost or misplaced.
— Some students lost interest very quickly, while others rose to the challenge and finished all their stories in two weeks, then had nothing left to do.
— Students quickly became bored with the follow-up activities for each story that seemed to do little more than measure literal-level comprehension.
— Students didn't seem to be learning anything—and I didn't seem to be teaching anything.
— I was no longer a teacher. Instead, I was endlessly managing the program, recording conferences, searching for lost stories and answer booklets, and doing general housekeeping chores to keep the kit in good shape.

The program didn't come to a screaming halt, but rather died in small stages over a period of a month or so—gone with a whimper not a bang. It became less cohesive by stages as students lost interest and I was unable to control it. I gave up the program, but kept the material in my classroom because the principal expected all of us to be involved in individualized reading education and the kit represented its essence. In other words, the presence of the kit showed that I was providing an individualized program for students and, to be truthful, I did use the materials in many different ways.

One of the problems with this program was that it asked teachers to make too many changes at once. We can't change our basic language-teaching approach, the way we make and keep records, the way students are expected to react and interact in the classroom, and the manner in which learning is managed and taught all at once without help.

The strategies and procedures discussed in the previous chapters are worthwhile. Some will work better than others and a particular strategy may work at one time and not another. Successfully implementing a new program is fairly simple—if we build on the skills and abilities students already possess and proceed cautiously, a step at a time. We need to learn to walk before we learn to run.

Our classrooms are not like the environments studied by emergent literacy researchers where the teacher-student ratio is often one-to-one. We must deal with a ratio of closer to thirty-to-one.

Nevertheless, we do have some choices:

— Teach the thirty-or-so students as a single group, forgetting their individual needs, interests and abilities.
— Teach them in three or four groups, still forgetting their individual needs, interests and abilities.
— Give up and become an administrator.
— Find out about cooperative learning and how it can be used to help phase in an integrated language program.

As we introduce integrated programs, the following universal educational laws are worth remembering:

— Nothing works as well in a real classroom as it does in the minds of educational writers and researchers (keep this in mind as you read on).
— The more radically we change our program, the more thoroughly prepared we and the students must be.
— In a program based on the concept that students should control their own learning, the teacher's role will vary from cooperative and useful to interfering and useless.
— If we're unable to control the behavior of thirty students involved in traditional drill-and-kill activities, the probability of succeeding in a holistic setting is close to zero.
— Good literature has a prominent place in an integrated program, but its purpose is *not* to teach students how to read.
— The program in our classrooms is ours alone—we design, implement, maintain, alter and adapt it. No prepackaged program exists, despite some publishers' claims to produce literature-based programs.
— As we introduce an integrated program, we may be viewed with suspicion and distrust by some of the students, some of the other teachers in the school and district, some administrators and some parents.
— The students themselves may represent the biggest obstacle to introducing an integrated program successful-

ly, especially if their schooling has been in traditional classrooms. For example, introducing writing to eleven- and twelve-year-olds from traditional classrooms is very difficult because they expect their work to be corrected, painfully rewritten, and graded by the teacher.

— There is no single route to an integrated, holistic program and no ideal model of such a program. Integrated instruction evolves and changes from day to day, week to week, and month to month as teachers, guided by our developing beliefs about learning, design and redesign the learning environment to support the ever-changing needs and interests of students within the limitations of the school and the resources that can be found, borrowed, bought or invented.

— A classroom program is only as good as the teacher's faith in it.

Traditional teachers often believe that students in holistic classrooms are allowed—and, indeed, encouraged—to explore their worlds without taking any responsibility, that they are neither asked nor expected to behave, that mayhem reigns, and that they are free to do just about anything they wish. This is far from the truth, though an individualized learning environment may *look* far more chaotic than a traditional classroom. Nevertheless, students are held accountable for learning and for a standard of conduct established by the teacher. They have a purpose, a direction and a goal. In effect, students will behave in the manner determined—either implicitly or explicitly—by the teacher.

The 10 Per Cent Solution

It is truly better to begin slowly, phasing in integrated activities and procedures, especially if the school year is already under way and a traditional program is operating fairly smoothly. A strategy that seems to work well is to begin with activities that involve all students in doing the same thing at the same time, then progress to independent learning activities. Those interested in trying a more comprehensive approach can skip to the section titled "Going Whole Hog."

No matter what happens, be patient. Some of the most superb teachers I know have taken as long as five years to implement an integrated program fully. This is not surprising because every program is different, based on the teacher's skills, needs and beliefs about what should be learned and the resources available, as well as the needs, interests and abilities of the particular students in the class.

SUSTAINED SILENT READING

Sustained silent reading (SSR), sometimes known as uninterrupted sustained silent reading (USSR), can provide an important stepping stone to integrated reading and writing activities. During SSR periods, students silently read books they have selected themselves.

The most vital feature of SSR is the teacher's attitude. SSR doesn't just happen. It must be nurtured and maintained by a teacher who is convinced of the importance of silent reading. This means ensuring that SSR time is inviolable. No one—not the principal, the custodian, the secretary, visiting parents or anyone else—is allowed to interrupt. This may involve posting a sign warning that no interruptions will be permitted. On days when it really is impossible to hold SSR, the teacher communicates his distress and disappointment to the class. This tells students that he values reading and the SSR period.

When SSR programs fail, it's often because teachers view the time as an opportunity to do things like correcting papers. Keep in mind that we are models for students. If we expect them to love to read, we must show them what loving to read looks like. Just as children who see their parents reading and enjoying it are more likely to enjoy reading, those who see their teacher reading and enjoying it are more likely to do so themselves. This pays valuable dividends, for students who enjoy reading are more likely to succeed in other areas of the curriculum.

The SSR period is a chance for us to read children's books so that we can be informed readers capable of talking to students about what they're reading. If we sit at the front of the class as we read, we can monitor students' behavior, finding out things like who has a book that's too difficult or who seems uninterested in the book she has selected.

SSR periods are frequently held for ten or fifteen minutes after lunch every day. They can be introduced by showing a new book to the group and, perhaps, reading a few paragraphs. Then, give the book to an interested child. Encourage the students, too, to pass along books they've enjoyed.

What happens at the end of SSR time is as important as what happens during SSR. Take a few minutes at the end of each session to focus on responding positively to books. For example, invite a volunteer to try to "sell" a book by presenting a brief book talk, then giving the book to another student.

Remember, as adult readers, we rarely write about books we've enjoyed. Instead, we tend to do oral reports. While it's certainly a good idea for students to keep a written log of books they've read, this shouldn't become another unwelcome chore. A simple record like the following works well:

Book Log

Name			
Title	Author	Date	Recommendation

Because interesting books must be readily available, a classroom library is important to successful SSR programs. A science-fiction center, a ghost-story center, a young-women's story center, a sports-story center and so on can be set up. While some of these will support integrated thematic programs, others will simply provide students with materials geared to their particular interests. If the prospect of developing a library is daunting, remember that parents are often willing to loan or donate materials.

SSR is a time when the class is actively involved and interested in reading as a group. Here are some of the obvious and less obvious benefits of SSR:

— When teachers enjoy reading, students see that books can be interesting and enjoyable. As the classroom interest library develops, they will become caught up in selecting books that interest them.
— Students will see reading as an integral part of the teacher's life as an adult.
— SSR is a quiet period that helps students focus their attention on reading in a reader-friendly environment.
— SSR often has a calming effect, focusing students' attention onto thinking and away from physical movement.

- SSR shows that quiet reflective activities are productive, positive and valuable.
- SSR encourages students to use their imaginations and visualize.
- SSR is a time when the teacher stops talking to students.
- SSR time encourages students to consider the value of introspective activities.
- SSR is a period when students can think for themselves.

Of course, there will always be students who see SSR as an opportunity to goof off or act out. I've taught in schools where there were a large number of troubled students who initially found SSR difficult for various complex reasons. In most cases, I discovered that if I found material that interested them, they spent the time at least perusing, if not actually reading, it. If I was able to involve them in the discussions at the end of the period, they were even more interested in participating in SSR.

While finding the right material wasn't always easy, high-interest materials do exist. In some cases, simple picture dictionaries fill the bill, perhaps because they show so many common objects in fascinating detail. In fact, some picture dictionaries are bilingual, making them perfect for ESL students to explore in their own first language. Oxford University Press produces several of these that even non-readers often find fascinating.

Students who need extra support can listen to a taped version of a book on headphones. Often, these students can progress from reading wordless picture books, including picture dictionaries, to predictable texts, to more complex texts.

Special Libraries for Special People

Evidence suggests that the English-language skills of ESL students who read good books in their first language at school don't suffer and, indeed, may benefit. Ken Walters, a colleague at Strathcona Elementary School in Vancouver, and I conducted a study in which we selected adults trained to be proficient oral readers in both English and Chinese. We found that their English achievement was not negatively affected by their experiences with Chinese books. In fact, the library circulation records of those involved in the study skyrocketed.

How can teachers develop a library for Mandarin-, Spanish- or Vietnamese-speaking students? Families are often willing to lend or donate books in the children's first language. In addition, many school and public libraries now have special shelves containing materials in languages other than English.

READING ALOUD

Young children love snuggling up to their parents, often at bedtime, to hear a story read aloud. Older students, too, enjoy listening to stories. I've seen students as old as eighteen looking forward to the daily ten minutes set aside by their teacher to read aloud a story. The sessions provide a shared experience for a class and often help students make the transition between activities. They're a time when students' attention focuses on the teacher and the class functions as a single team.

The 20 Per Cent Solution

SSR and reading stories aloud are powerful activities that already take place in many classrooms and represent important first steps towards developing integrated programs. For many teachers, introducing holistic writing activities that involve keeping logs is the next logical step.

Writing that is natural and meaningful is an important element of holistic programs. Learning logs and teacher-student cooperative logs were described earlier in the chapter titled, "Why, What, When, How?"

The cooperative log represents a conversation or discussion between the teacher and students. The teacher makes no comments on issues relating to mechanics; rather she focuses on what the students are saying. Many teachers schedule about ten minutes at the end of the day at least twice a week for students to make their log entries, which may include notes and questions about what they're doing and feeling. It's an opportunity for students to explore and think about their learning. The teacher responds in writing to each student. While this may sound time-consuming, I've found that it takes no longer than correcting thirty worksheets.

Like sustained silent reading, the time devoted to making log entries involves all students in working independently at the same time.

In many respects, introducing and maintaining logs with older students is more difficult than with younger students.

Typically, older students associate writing with "school work." They have learned—and, indeed, expect—that their writing will be scrutinized, marked up and graded. For this reason, it's a good idea to explain carefully—and demonstrate—that keeping a log is different.

To introduce log-writing and help students understand what's expected, ask them to write in cooperative logs for ten minutes at the end of every day for two weeks. Initially, you might discuss the kinds of things they may wish to write and the range of issues you will respond to. Read their entries, write your comments and return the logs the next day. After this, making entries two or three times a week is often enough.

Just as it's important for students to see adults interested in and enjoying reading, it's important for them to see their teacher interested in and enjoying writing. Keep your own log, making entries at the same time as students. Help them feel comfortable reading aloud their own material and listening as others read theirs. In a supportive environment, students often come to love writing and do so with a vengeance.

Some teachers establish a regular period for sustained silent writing (SSW), conducted in much the same way as SSR sessions. The teacher models interest in and enjoyment of writing, talks about his own writing and encourages students to do the same. He may also identify writing he wishes to publish and suggest things that students may wish to publish.

SSR, SSW and cooperative logs can be the beginnings of a whole language program. When it seems appropriate, teacherrs can gradually introduce some of the whole-class activities described in the two preceding chapters. The next step is to begin phasing in independent, individual learning activities.

Basketball Is a Nice Game!

So far, we've discussed only activities that involve students in working independently at the same thing at the same time. In these situations, the teacher is like a symphony conductor, directing and encouraging students to work independently at whole-group activities. Now, it's time for the teacher to assume the role of coach by engaging students in cooperative learning—activities in which each child completes a specific task that helps a small group achieve a common goal.

Begin by dividing the class into groups of four or five and arrange the classroom so that group members can sit together facing each other as they would at a dinner table.

The makeup of the groups is important. It's a good idea to avoid traditional ability groups—don't place all the "good" readers in one group and all the "poor" readers in another. Interest groups work well if the numbers are convenient. Some teachers balance the groups with different kinds of "personalities," while others include students with a range of abilities—a high achiever, a low achiever, and two or three students in between. Research has shown that this kind of grouping results in superior cooperative learning.

Each group member is assigned a task—timekeeper, recorder, reporter, expediter or guide, and reactor (an optional role). Initially, the teacher usually assigns the duties but, as students become used to working cooperatively, they may choose their own roles.

The timekeeper's task is to keep track of the time limit established for the activity and let the group know how much time is left. A large classroom clock is helpful. Timekeepers may require some practice at participating in the group discussion while keeping track of the time.

The recorder makes notes and is responsible for seeing that written tasks are completed and presented to the teacher or the class as a whole.

The expediter or guide helps keep the group on task, establish who does what, and track the group's tasks and goals.

Because cooperative group activities work best when everyone has a task, the fifth member—if there is one—is the reactor, whose job is to report to the group how well he or she thinks the group is fulfilling its task. While the guide might make comments like, "We have to come up with a list of insects," the reactor might ask, "Are these names of insects?"

At first, the cooperative learning tasks should be kept as simple as possible so that each group member has a chance to participate and fulfill his or her responsibilities.

Typically, the teacher might introduce the task by saying, "Here are the instructions for your group task. First, timers, this will be a three-minute task. When I say go, you'll have three minutes exactly. At the end of three minutes, everyone in the group will raise a hand to signal that you're finished. Recorders, your list should be on a single piece of lined paper with each item numbered. Reporters, you'll read your list aloud to the class when I ask you. Guides, your group's task is to brainstorm and come up with a list of as many harmful insects as you can. If you have any questions, please raise your hand. Reactors, remember that your job is to let the group know how well you're doing.

"Okay, let me see the hands of those who understand what they're to do. That's great, everyone's ready. Look at the clock, timers. It's fifteen seconds to 9:30. We'll begin at 9:30 exactly. Ready? Go."

If students are inexperienced at working cooperatively in groups, the instructions can be written on the chalkboard or a chart. At the end of the prescribed time, each reporter reads the group's list. At this point, the teacher provides positive feedback by saying things like, "The cooperative task went very well. I was impressed with the way the Ninjas worked. Tommy kept them informed of the time every fifteen seconds and also contributed his own ideas. They lowered their voices and got closer together so they could work more efficiently. They didn't try to compete with each other and really co-operated to come up with a list of thirty-eight insects."

If students are having trouble keeping on task, it may be necessary at first to offer some sort of extrinsic reward, such as points. As students become better at functioning in small groups and learning cooperatively, the tasks assigned can become more complex and longer. It is possible, for instance, to assign a group the task of researching and writing a report on the effects of pollution on the world's weather.

Knowledge searches, too, are ideally suited for small group activities. For example, a teacher who decides that it's important for students to learn about harmful insects might prepare a study guide asking questions that can't be answered by referring to a single information source. Each group is given the study guide, the questions are reviewed and the groups are challenged to answer them within a given time limit, such as forty-five minutes. Because this is, of course, not enough time for any single group member to complete the task, students must cooperate. In this case, because all the groups are asked to complete the task in the library at the same time, it becomes even more difficult. Inter- and intra-group cooperation and coordination are necessary.

This kind of cooperation requires students to abide by the following rules, which should be discussed beforehand:

— Materials cannot be hoarded.
— Each student will be graded based on one report written by each group.
— Any student in any group may be asked to answer any question on the study guide. This means that each student must know all the answers. The most efficient way to achieve this is usually for the groups to reserve time near the end of the allotted period to discuss questions and answers.
— Infractions of the rules will be considered when the groups are evaluated.

As the dynamic of the groups becomes evident, it may be necessary to alter their membership. Some teachers do this regularly at one-month or six-week intervals, anyway. If students are organized into interest groups, be aware that interest and ability are sometimes related. For example, the overall reading ability of students in a science-fiction group may be quite different from that of students in a skateboarding group.

At this stage, the teacher continues to control much of the students' learning. Independent learning doesn't just happen—it requires practice. Groups will function more smoothly if students are experienced at groupwork and the teacher has explicitly discussed each member's role. Acting as a coach, it's important for the teacher to describe how students are working together and identify the skills they already possess as well as those they need to practice.

If the ultimate purpose of the cooperative groups is limited to filling out worksheets, this kind of cooperative learning can be as mechanistic as other traditional classroom activities. On the other hand, if they are viewed as an important stepping stone to developing an integrated, individualized program, they can help students make the transition to independent learning and provide the teacher with a crucial tool to help plan, initiate, maintain and evaluate the process.

In addition to the cooperative activities described in this section, many of the activities suggested in earlier chapters are appropriate for group work.

It's ironic that students are seldom consulted when teachers plan learning programs for them. This is unfortunate, for students who feel a sense of ownership over their learning are likely to learn more efficiently and enthusiastically. By including them in at least some of the planning, we can foster this sense of control. I've seen students from five to fourteen years old successfully involved in helping plan learning programs.

The basic approach is straightforward. The teacher begins by selecting two or three broad areas or themes—pollution, ecology, communication, insects or energy production, for example—that students either must or should learn about. It's also a good idea to survey the school library to make sure the areas selected are well-supported by resource materials.

The teacher then presents the themes to the class, inviting students to help decide which they want to study. At this point, some teachers ask students to suggest broad themes themselves. If students are unfamiliar with a topic, it may be necessary to describe it before inviting them to make a choice.

Let's assume that students have decided that they want to learn more about communication. Invite groups to brainstorm to produce a list of sub-topics that might be included in the overall theme. The following list was generated in ten minutes by groups of eleven- and twelve-year-olds. I wrote the items on the chalkboard as each reporter read the group's list aloud.

Communication

Newspapers	Talking	Listening	Television
Radio	Telephones	Writing	Storytelling
Records	Books	Logs	Diaries
Music	Video-disks	Tapes	Reading
Singing	Painting	Street signs	Letters
Notes	Sign language	Braille	PA system
Sharing	Chalkboard	Letters	Pictures
Logos	Pens	Pencils	Computers
Typewriters	Brushes	Spray paint	Satellites
Faxes	Totem poles	Cartoons	Gossip
Plays	Mime	Teachers	Parents
Concerts	Meetings	Conferences	Playing
Games	Horns	Whistles	Bells
Speedometers	Gauges	Thermometers	Road marks

Footprints	Claw marks	Paths	Faces
Sounds	Wind	Stars	Clouds
Makeup	Opera	Movies	Code

The students in this particular class were experienced co-operative learners who provided an impressive rationale for including every item they reported.

The next task was to organize the items to make planning easier. As a class, the students decided that five areas were interesting and worth further study—newspapers, television, radio, computers and writing systems. Two groups independently considered newspapers while each of the other topics was considered by a single group. The groups were asked to produce a web indicating possible areas of study and a list of questions to be answered. Students worked on this activity for about forty minutes, interrupted by a fifteen-minute recess break. The following web was produced by the TV group:

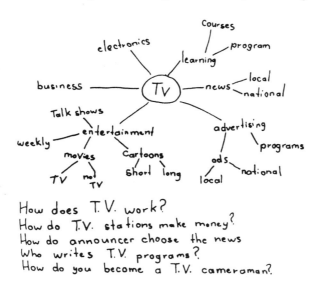

How does T.V. work?
How do T.V. stations make money?
How do announcer choose the news
Who writes T.V. programs?
How do you become a T.V. cameraman?

I collected and contemplated the webs and questions before making a list of items that could be used to help students learn about the areas they had identified. Each of the five webs contributed significantly to the general theme and could be developed as a six- or eight-week unit of study. I chose to develop each as a learning center and involved the groups in developing each center.

Each group reviewed its web and developed a list of materials and resources that would be useful in studying the theme. All the groups concluded that the information available in the classroom was too limited, making a visit to the school library essential. The teacher-librarian was consulted and scheduled time for us to visit the library where she had set up an information table that included a list of the audio-visual materials available at our local educational media center. The groups were challenged to come up with a specific list of available materials that would contribute to their study. They were also asked to develop an inventory of vital materials that they couldn't find in the library or the media center catalogue. We then visited the community public library where we developed similar lists.

I used the surveys to begin to plan and collect materials for five learning centers. Each center was designed after I had reviewed the student-generated surveys. I assessed the available materials and surveyed other sources. Then I invited each group to help set up and arrange its own center.

The TV center, for example, included material on the electronics of television transmission, the technology and machinery of television production, television advertising, news collection and broadcasting, television financing and production techniques. One of the most popular activities turned out to be writing and producing TV commercials. Other activities included answering the questions generated by the cooperative groups in worksheet form, evaluating TV commercials, interviewing individuals in the school and producing a fifteen-minute television news report, and producing surveys of the products advertised on the local station. Activities like those outlined in the previous chapter were designed to encourage students to become critical comprehenders of the material they see on television. One survey activity, by the way, found that early Saturday-morning television concentrated on advertising costly toys, most of them quite violent.

This cooperative planning venture involved students in deciding what interested them and what areas they wanted to study, surveying the resources available in the school, the community library, their homes and the community, and helping set up the centers. Each of these was an interesting learning activity. My role was to find additional resources, coordinate activities, and help set up the classroom so that the centers could function independently. Each group worked as a group at each center, maximizing cooperation. The next step is to encourage students to work totally independently.

Critics might say that involving students in this kind of organizing and planning effectively surrenders the teacher's responsibilities. After all, taxpayers pay teachers to teach.

In fact, involving students in planning and implementing their own learning represents the ultimate in learning. As a teacher, I learn more about a particular subject by researching, planning and developing learning activities or centers than I do by reading texts and worksheets. Students, too, learn more when they're actively involved in the planning and implementation than when they simply read prepared materials and complete teacher-prepared activities. Cooperative group planning, with the teacher acting as guide and expediter, helps students take control of their own learning.

Who's on First?

In addition to helping plan their own learning, students can also help manage their own programs. Many authors suggest that students maintain portfolios of their work that can be used for assessment purposes. In *Writing Portfolios*, for example, Sandra Murphy and Mary Ann Smith suggest that maintaining portfolios helps students become active partners in fostering their own growth as writers. And Robert Tierney proposed to a conference that students behave like artists, selecting their best work—writing they especially liked, taped oral reading sessions, etc.—to include in their portfolios.

Students can also be invited to maintain a learning checklist, a kind of book-keeping journal that includes them in the management and record-keeping that an integrated program requires.

When airline pilots prepare to take off, they consult a checklist. Indeed, it is the copilot's duty to read aloud the checklist and confirm that the items have been looked after. While the pilot is in charge, she is guided by the items on the checklist read by the copilot. When the flight is nearly over and the pilot is preparing to land the plane, a checklist is consulted again.

Similarly, a learning checklist helps guide students to maintain their writing-reading portfolios, ensuring that they have conferences with the teacher, are involved in learning activities, have completed and turned in work, and maintained the different kinds of logs included in their program.

Many teachers schedule checklist periods at the beginning of the day—to discover activities that need attending to—and at the end of the day as a kind of record-keeping period in which students select items for their portfolios and assess how well they've succeeded in completing the planned activities.

Some teachers use a general checklist while others provide a daily checklist tailored to each group's studies in different interest areas. In one class, for instance, the checklists for groups studying dinosaurs and ecology were quite different because they were involved in different learning activities.

Checklist periods are conducted in much the same way as other cooperative group activities, depending upon the students' expertise in cooperative functioning, with the teacher providing explicit directions and outcomes.

The following is a generic checklist designed to be filled out by individual students in a group setting. Each group's guide was instructed to read each item, giving group members time to record and make notations on their individual checklists. The reporter was then asked to make certain the completed checklists and associated materials were placed in a designated spot. The "work box" refers to a container in which students store their completed work. These containers are kept in a central location where the teacher can monitor individual students' progress and assess individual work activities. Library pocket cards are quite handy for this purpose because they are portable, can be easily labeled and are fairly inexpensive.

Checklist

1. Comments have been written in your student-teacher log and the log is included in your work box. _____

2. New material has been written in your writing log and the log is included in your work box. _____

3. Books you have finished reading have been recorded in your reading log and the log is included in your work box. _____

4. Finished math work ready for correction has been put in your work box.   _____

5. Completed special projects have been included in your work box.   _____

6. Completed ecology center work has been included in your work box.   _____

7. Completed science center work has been included in your work box.   _____

8. Completed television center work has been included in your work box.   _____

9. Writing for publication has been included in your work box.   _____

10. Edited and rewritten work has been submitted to the word processing center.   _____

11. Have you selected any work you want to include in your portfolio? Is it in your portfolio?   _____

12. Check if you have had a conference with the teacher.   _____
    What was the outcome of the conference?

    _____

Checklists can be kept in a variety of formats. The one on the following page is typical. In some ways, it resembles a traditional grade book; however, it applies to only one student who maintains his own record. Keeping records this way enables teachers to consider each student individually.

While completing checklists takes time, it's more efficient for students to keep their own records than for the teacher to keep track of everything. If students are experienced at working in cooperative groups, they'll have no trouble participating in this kind of record-keeping. Even checklists for primary students, while they may involve less detail, can be as informative as those designed for older students.

If students maintain portfolios, collections of work they feel represent their efforts, the checklist period provides time for them to consider their work, discuss their choices with other students and assemble their portfolio collections.

Individual Checklist

Name						Month				
	M	T	W	T	F	M	T	W	T	F
Reading										
Assignment										
Conference										
Shared Reading										
Log										
Writing										
Log										
Special Project										
S-T Log										
Publishing										
-Rewrite										
-Published										
Math										
Assignment										
Project										
Workbook										

C—Completed   NH—Need Help
IP—(In Progress) Working on It   N—No   R—Rewriting

Checklists streamline classroom management and assessment. I once used checklists filled out by the seven- and eight-year-olds in my class to produce a weekly report that was sent home Friday afternoon and returned, signed by a parent, on Monday morning. This wasn't as difficult as it sounds because the checklists meant that the children helped keep the records. Parents loved the weekly reports because they always knew what their children were doing, what needed to be completed, and how they were improving.

The checklists helped the children keep track of what needed to be completed and encouraged them to take responsibility for their own learning and work habits.

Cooperative groups help teachers and students explore and design areas of study, survey resources, create and set up learning centers, and assess progress. In addition, my experience indicates that cooperative groups are the most efficient way to manage an individualized program, especially in the early stages. Of course, the goal is to eliminate group management and assessment activities in favor of encouraging students to contribute independently to the process.

Going Whole Hog

If students are to be involved in independent holistic learning, care and planning are essential. While it is not within the scope of this book to provide a detailed discussion of either individualized programs or the integration of reading and writing into content subjects, both must be considered when preparing an integrated reading and writing program.

The following checklist outlines items that require consideration. Items that may be unfamiliar are marked with asterisks and explained in more detail in the material that follows.

A Program Checklist

The classroom contains...

1. A collection of books that takes into account, at least in part, students' varied interests. _____

2. A work box for each student where work can be stored and turned in to the teacher as a unit. _____

3. Portfolios to hold a variety of materials such as written compositions and audio- or videotapes for each student. _____

4. At least four centers that have clearly identified learning activities. _____

5. A book log for each student. _____

6. A writing log for each student. _____

7. A student-teacher reaction log for each student. _____

8. A conference log listing students in order. _____

9. An ample supply of conference reports. _____

10. A large sign—or signs—saying, SSR PERIOD—DO NOT DISTURB! for posting on classroom doors. _____

11. A word processing center to assist students in publishing written work. _____

12. A recording center where students can record oral reading samples. _____

13. A parental aide. _____

14. A classroom library that features students' published work. _____

15. Collections of high-interest materials. _____

16. A newsletter that explains the program to parents, other teachers and the school administrator.* _____

17. Individual learning development checklist. (See next chapter.) _____

18. Individual diagnostic language assessment forms. _____ (See next chapter)

19. Teacher's management clipboard.* _____

20. A library card from the closest public library. _____

21. Free delivery of a copy of the community news-paper for each student once a week. _____

22. A first-language library, possibly borrowed from the parents of ESL students. _____

23. Parents who are trained to be good oral readers of children's books. _____

24. Math, social studies, science, physical education, and social and cultural awareness activities that take into account individual differences and are integrated into the language learning activities. _____

25. A reading interest inventory. _____

26. A content reading inventory for each of the con-ent books you intend to use. _____

27. A mechanism for recording and reporting students' progress in a manner meaningful to them and their parents. _____

28. A reflective evaluation form for students.* _____

Students...

1. Who understand your teaching and learning philosophy. _____

2. Who know how to maintain a reading log. _____

3. Who know how to maintain a student-teacher reaction log. _____

4. Who know how to work independently. _____

   a. Where to find materials. _____

   b. How to select portfolio materials. _____

   c. How to get help from you. _____

   d. How to maintain a checklist. _____

   e. How to plan time. _____

   f. How to learn independently. _____

5. Who know how to participate in conferences. _____

6. Who know their own responsibilities all the time. _____

You, the teacher...

1. Are aware that integrated learning programs are complex and require considerable organization. ____

2. Are an enthusiastic and knowledgeable reader. _____

3. Are an enthusiastic and knowledgeable writer. _____

4. Are an exceptional resource developer and discoverer. _____

5. Enjoy learning. _____

6. Know that you are in charge of the classroom learning environment and that your main goal is to empower students to take control of their own learning. _____

7. Know that teaching is political and that you may have to defend your program against criticism from others with a more traditional view of teaching and learning. _____

8. Know the local public librarian well and can ask for his or her assistance. _____

9. Have a close professional relationship with the school librarian. _____

10. Know that the students' physical and emotional well-being is one of your primary responsibilities and that this may require you to impose your will on students at particular times. _____

PARENT NEWSLETTER

Students, principals, neighboring teachers and, most of all, parents need to be informed about changes in students' learning activities. While school-based individuals can be contacted directly, parents are sometimes harder to get in touch with. Yet, parents need to know about the program and the theoretical foundations upon which it is based. A newsletter serves a double function—it explains the program and activities and presents examples of students' work.

Newsletters are sometimes a pain to produce, but they do provide important information to parents. They explain why their children may bring home work that is not corrected with red pencil in the traditional fashion. They show that the program is based on the thoughtful application of research in learning. They anticipate and answer parental concerns.

A quarterly newsletter seems to work well, although I've seen weekly newsletters produced successfully in senior elementary classrooms in Alberta and California. In these cases, the students took over the task of producing the newsletters. The teacher's job was to provide an information column.

STUDENTS' REFLECTIVE EVALUATION

Students must—and should—know many things in language arts and reading. Teachers are responsible for ensuring that students learn useful, meaningful skills and develop their abilities. They are professionals who know what students should learn. The curriculum imposed by teachers' guides produced by commercial publishers and in the mandates handed down by official curriculum committees ignores the classroom teacher's expertise in assessing the needs, interests and abilities of particular students in a particular classroom. Only the classroom teacher understands what individual students know, need to know, should know, and want to know.

Because holistic programs focus on process rather than product, teachers take control of the curriculum and encourage students to participate in decisions about their own learning. Students learn what they and their teachers believe is important and meaningful. Taking control of the curriculum also means that teachers assume responsibility for monitoring individual students' development. This requires keeping meticulous records, including anecdotal observations. The teacher keeps track of students' learning and plans further learning, taking into account their needs, interests and abilities.

In traditional settings, evaluation focuses on the teacher's assessment of how well students have learned. In most cases, traditional report cards show the teacher's evaluation of the "work" students have completed—or not, as the case may be—over a specified period. Oddly, the people who know the most about students' learning—the students themselves—are rarely invited to contribute.

Holistic teachers often encourage students to participate in the evaluation process by reflecting on their own learning. This can take a variety of forms. It can be general, a reflection on overall progress during a given period, or specific, a look at what was accomplished during, for example, a six-week theme study. The evaluations may be guided by the teacher, who lists what students are expected to assess, or they may be open-ended, with the students selecting the items they wish to focus on. Even primary children can participate, using happy faces to indicate their assessment.

This kind of evaluation doesn't eliminate the need for a "report card." Rather, it adds important information to the evaluation process. It encourages students to reflect on their own progress, abilities, achievements and needs, sometimes revealing information that teachers didn't know. Overall, it can tell teachers how a class perceives its learning activities. The following form is designed to help students evaluate their progress in general terms after a specified period:

Individual Evaluation Form

Name		
Date		
Evaluation Scale: E—Excellent VG—Very Good G—Good S—Satisfactory F—Fair NH—Needs Help		
Area	Evaluation	Reflection
Math		
Science		
Social studies		
Spelling		
Phys. ed.		
Writing		
Reading		

TEACHER'S MANAGEMENT CLIPBOARD

In fully individualized, integrated learning programs, teachers interact with individual students at different times in different ways during the school day. A management clipboard is a vital record that helps teachers keep track of the myriad details that emerge from these interactions, plan activities and guide students' learning. A typical clipboard is shown here.

Management Clipboard

Date				
Student	Needs	Wants	Find Out	Comments
J. Adams				
R. Bright				
B. Kuzyk				
R. Singh				
C. Schott				

As the day progresses, the teacher notes what individual students are doing, what they need, and what learning is taking place. At the end of every month, the twenty-or-so sheets provide information that can be used both to plan future activities and record students' learning.

Summary

This chapter has provided some ideas for gradually changing the classroom from one that involves the whole class in a single activity to one in which individual students pursue independent learning activities. It has recommended that the changes be systematic and well-thought-out. Independent integrated reading and writing programs are complex, requiring students both to participate in complex cooperative interactions and to work independently. They require a great deal of record-keeping, planning for individual learning, and one-to-one student-teacher interactions. Cooperative planning provides the teacher with a way of gradually initiating an individualized program and encourages students to begin to take charge of their own learning by helping with management procedures.

. . . .

IS AN "A" BY ANY OTHER
NAME AS SWEET?

People often treasure their old report cards. While these are interesting, the rows of A's, Bs, and Cs don't say very much. The comments, though, tell us more. "David is an excellent writer with an inventive imagination," says far more than a B+ in the composition column. Assessment is an integral part of day-to-day classroom activities. There is a great deal of contention, however, about what should be assessed—and how.

What Grade Did I Get?

The belief that standardized tests measure something worthwhile, are based on a solid scientific foundation and provide valuable information pervades any discussion of assessment. Many school districts report standardized test scores in community newspapers, often just as contract negotiations with teachers are about to begin.

In *Applied Linguistics*, Carol Edelsky and her colleagues said, "It is possible to become truly literate without enduring a school curriculum based on artificial pieces of discourse, pretend-functional print, and exercises that masquerade as literacy." They also note that "...there are children in schools which have begun to emphasize real literacy, who are 'false negatives', i.e. they do not test well although they have become literate through a continued emphasis on 'the real thing'...." No one becomes literate by filling in the bubbles in multiple-choice exercises, though this activity may certainly give students practice in taking standardized tests. Standardized tests are based on a notion of language that is dated, atomistic, simplistic and unfounded.

Students are wonderfully individual. We can't point to a single child and say, "This is a typical nine-year-old." No ready-made package adequately takes into account the variety found in a class of nine-year-olds. Human beings develop and learn according to their own individual patterns. No standard chronology describes an individual nine-year-old's learning sequence.

Another problem is that the people most concerned about students' progress—parents—are often left out of the learning process. Parents of preschoolers know everything about their child's development. They know how well he can read and write, whether he likes to read, write and talk, and what he thinks about learning. If asked, they can tell anyone what their child needs to know, in both the short and long terms.

Once their child enrolls in school, however, they begin to lose touch. They may ask, "What did you learn at school today?" but the answer usually isn't particularly helpful. While teachers can certainly do a better job of including parents by making schools more parent-friendly places, the economic realities of the 1990s make it unlikely that parental involvement will increase. Parents are already dealing with incredible demands on their time. As their instructional stand-ins, then, teachers must do a better job of providing them with learning evaluation and assessment information.

What's Her Level?

In addition to the belief that standardized tests actually mean something, another bit of folklore pervades education. People, even many otherwise knowledgeable professional educators, accept that grade-level or form designations also mean something. This is simply untrue. These designations are for the convenience of administrators who must place students somewhere. The belief that five-year-olds are ready to begin formal schooling is pure bunk. Sometimes they are—and sometimes they aren't.

How are seven- and eight-year-olds different from six- and seven-year-olds? Well, they're older, sometimes a little taller and heavier, often a bit more physically coordinated, perhaps slightly better at speaking, usually better able to deal with the bits and pieces of instruction we call language arts, and so on. But, while all this may be true *on average*, it may have very little to do with a particular six- or seven-year old.

This brings us to a question that has vexed researchers for a long time: how are books designated for second grade different from first-grade books? A simple answer is that they contain slightly longer words (in syllables) and sentences because publishers use readability formulas to make them different. But is a second-grade book really at the second-grade reading level? No one really knows for sure because:

— Second-grade level doesn't mean anything in particular.
— A first-grade book produced by one publisher may be as difficult as the second-grade book of another.
— Grades or forms are arbitrary categories constructed to represent someone of a particular age and ability level. This child doesn't really exist nor does the category.
— A second-grade designation represents an *average* estimation of a book's suitability. In fact, specific examination is likely to reveal a range of reading levels. Some will be easier than grade two and some more difficult.
— An individual student's background and motivation will make a so-called second-grade book too difficult in some cases and a fifth-grade book too easy in others.

Attempts to categorize children according to grade level or form should be abandoned. Ask a parent how her four-year-old is reading and she'll likely relate anecdotes about her interest, the number of books she reads, how well she understands, and what she wants to read next. The parent is unlikely to say that she's reading at a pre-primer or first-grade level.

Authentic Assessment

If standardized test scores and assigning levels are inaccurate reflections of students' skills and abilities, how do we assess their reading? How well does a ten-year-old read? How should a thirteen-year-old's writing be evaluated? What information does provide parents with an authentic assessment of their child's learning and development?

112

I once sat with a friend and reviewed her report cards for thirteen years of school. The A's, Bs and Cs didn't mean much to her, although they sometimes said something about her teachers. The comments meant the most—"Katherine's handwriting is beautiful...Katherine's poetry is wonderful. She should be encouraged to write more...Katherine seems to have difficulty with written math problems...Katherine has an exceptional talent for working with younger children." These were honest, authentic assessments.

How do we authentically assess reading and writing? Authentic assessment requires teachers to be completely familiar with a student's development and performance over time. How do teachers find out about how a student reads? We watch her read. We keep a record of what she reads—actually, she can do this herself. We record her reading orally. We talk to her about what she's reading, gauging her enthusiasm and interest. We assess her understanding of content texts by monitoring her participation in group activities and through the learning she demonstrates in the activities she completes.

But what about the reading skills adults take for granted, such as the ability to decode words phonetically? Informal reading assessments provide fairly detailed information about a student's reading abilities. Much information can be obtained by observing students carefully during the school day. Clipboard notes, mentioned in the previous chapter, are invaluable information sources, an essential part of the program. Further, a great deal of information about students' general language development, including reading, can be gained from assessing their writing development.

In his classic long-term study of language development, Walter Loban observed, "Although instruction cannot transcend maturation very far, it can increase language proficiency...the influence of the school can be favorable or unfavorable...A curriculum which respects the child's stage of readiness for learning language is particularly important."

Loban tracked 220 students over ten years and found that listening and speaking are the "foundations of proficiency" in the other language skills and that there are "clear and positive relationships" among language abilities. In other words, there is a very high positive relationship between reading and writing ability, between speaking and reading ability and so on.

Several years ago, a veteran first-grade teacher contacted my colleague, Jon Shapiro, and me to help assess the writing of the children in her class to discover whether they were, in fact, learning basic skills, such as phonics, and the sight words many authorities believe it's important to master. Mrs. R had abandoned the basal readers prescribed by the provincial education ministry and her school board in favor of process writing, a literature-based reading program, and individualized instruction focusing on the children's interests.

On the first day of the school year, these six- and seven-year-olds were given writing logs and invited to write. Jon and I collected and copied everything they wrote over the year. We continued to collect samples of their writing, by the way, until the end of third grade. Our attempts to analyze and assess their writing development taught us a great deal.

There were, of course, wide variations in these youngsters' writing ability and interest when they started school. The immediate introduction of writing logs sparked a range of actions and reactions. Some children said they couldn't write, some drew pictures, some produced lines of letters and letter-like shapes, some produced recognizable words, and a few wrote readable texts. Our challenge was to come up with a way of assessing these attempts.

Researchers have suggested that young children pass through the following stages as they learn to write:

— Pictures.
— Scribbling.
— Letter strings (random).
— Letter strings with occasional phonic hits.
— Letter strings with spaces between "words," some phonic hits.
— Letter strings, words, phonic hits, invented spellings.
— Sentences, invented and traditional spellings, some punctuation and capitalization.
— Sentences, traditional and some invented spellings, traditional punctuation and capitalization, paragraphs.

Our analyses indicated that all these stages were represented in the children's writing. In fact, the writing of a single child often included characteristics typical of several different phases. As the year progressed, the children began to produce more and more readable texts, some of them evolving from three- to five-word single sentences to 3,000-word, multiple-sentence, structurally sophisticated and complex narratives.

In addition to analyzing the children's writing, we were also interested in observing the development of their vocabulary, spelling and knowledge of phonics. We used a computer to rank lists of words according to the frequency of their appearance. We found that the children were learning basic vocabulary similar to that introduced in basal readers. We also found, by analyzing their invented spellings, that they were learning phonics, although traditional phonics lessons were not part of their instructional program.

When we conducted this study, we were keenly aware of Kellogg Hunt's contention, outlined in *Grammatical Structures Written at Three Grade Levels*, that children younger than nine are simply not ready to write. Of course, his study involved observing students in traditional classrooms where the notion that writing instruction should come after reading instruction was firmly established in the minds of the teachers. In fact, the first-graders in Mrs. R's class outperformed the fourth-graders in Hunt's study on all fronts.

This graph shows the mean number of words produced per writing product by all the children over the course of the year:

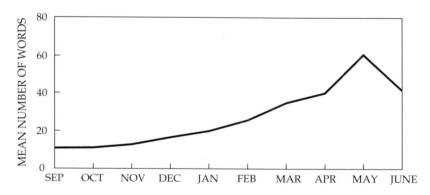

The following is a list of correctly spelled words in order of frequency from most to least (read across the columns from left to right). This was valuable information because it told Mrs. R that the children were learning to spell the high-frequency words fundamental to basal reading programs.

| the | of | and | a |
| to | in | is | you |

that	it	he	for
was	on	are	as
with	his	they	at
be	this	from	I
have	or	by	one
had	not	but	what
were	we	there	can
an	your		

The following is a list of invented spellings produced by the students as a group:

when—wen, wan, whan wene
girl—gril, grl
too—to
was—wuz, wos
there—thar, ther, tar, der
now—naw
that—tat, thet
know—no
some—sum
house—hos, hous
to—too
found—fond
made—mad
came—cam
bought—bot
have—hav
the—th
coming—comeing
name—nam
father—fother
fight—fite
make—mak
so—sow
woman—women

their—there, ther
will—wil
like—lik
they—thay
man—mon
would—wod, wood, wold
said—siad, sed
saw—so, sow
called—cold
one—oun
white—wit
home—hom
back—bak, bac, bake
then—thin, than
get—git, gat
put—pot, poot
went—wet
ground—grond
out—owt
his—hes
build—bild
nice—nis
two—to, too
birds—brids

An examination of these spellings revealed to Mrs. R that, as a group, the children were learning phonics and the rules of English orthography. Although they might misapply a rule from time to time (e.g., writing "cride" for "cried"), they were nevertheless using their knowledge of phonics to come up with logical spellings. As the sophistication of their knowledge increased, they began to distinguish among the rules and apply them correctly.

While these analyses provided interesting and important information about the group's learning, they gave Mrs. R no information about individual students. Over the course of the study, then, I became interested in developing procedures enabling teachers to assess writing development, vocabulary, spelling and knowledge of phonics on an individual basis.

After a great deal of experimentation, I found that randomly selecting one writing sample a week for each student and analyzing it in the computer database provided a reliable picture of writing and vocabulary development over the school year. The analysis revealed that the writing development of individual students resembled that of the group. This graph outlines the average number of words used by one ESL student in each writing product over the course of a year.

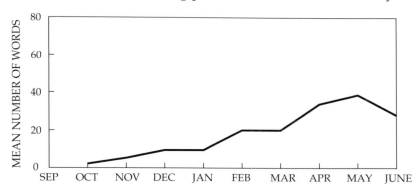

The following is a list of the words the same student used over the year ranked according to frequency (read from left to right):

and	I	the	to
is	my	it	a
am	then	with	in
we	man	going	he
playing	old	was	are
me	gingerbread	of	saw
she	her	said	you
from	he-man	now	Wai Chi
ran	some	toys	after
have	house	an	away

By the end of the school year, we had analyzed more than 2,000 writing products and 150,000 words. Busy classroom teachers don't have the time required for a detailed study like this. Furthermore, our analysis was conducted on a mainframe computer, something unavailable to most teachers.

What Parents Really Ought to Know

Parents freely give friends and relatives reports on their children's development, including how they're doing in reading and writing—with only an occasional proud exaggeration of the truth. Here's what a parent's report might sound like:

> "Jimmy's reading Dr. Seuss. He can't get enough of Dr. Seuss's books. His favorite is *Green Eggs and Ham.* He started reading when he was about three. You should see his writing. Look at this—a note asking Daddy to get him some new tennis balls. The way he wrote 'tens blls' for tennis balls was cute. I think he's doing great for a five-year-old. He loves books so much we have trouble getting him enough new ones."

This report is much more informative than many of the report cards filled with letter grades that are regularly sent home to parents. Our reporting to parents can become more informative by including dated and chronologically representative work samples selected by the teacher and the student, including taped oral reading samples, anecdotal notations, writing logs, a collection of checklists, reading and writing inventories, content inventories, interest inventories, self-appraisal results and developmental writing analyses.

If this material were sent home to parents, part of an end-of-year assessment written by the teacher might read like this:

> Patty began school writing stories that were about forty words long. Her stories were short and not very well-developed. I scored her stories at about a seven on the nine-point scale included in this folder of work. In September, she used many invented spellings, although she correctly spelled important high-frequency words like "the" and "come." As the printout shows, her stories have improved so that now she writes about 200 words for each essay and her writing is at about eight-plus on

118

the holistic scoring scale. Her invented spellings—notice she spelled astronaut as "astrunawt" and aquatic as "ekwatic"—show that she is developing a good understanding of phonics. The list of words she spells correctly shows that she has a good spelling vocabulary.

At the beginning of the year, the content-reading inventory showed that Patty had trouble handling some content-area reading skills. When she took the assessment again in May, you can see her skills had improved.

She was not very interested in reading in September, as you can see from the comments in her log and from the results of an interest inventory. Her reading log, however, shows that she has gone from reading one book a month in September to one book a week in May and June. Her self-appraisal also reveals she is much more interested in reading, especially books about horses. Her last self-appraisal and my observations show that Patty still has some trouble with using quotation marks in text.

Compiling a report like this is not as difficult as it might seem because the material is collected and assessed by both the students and the teacher over the course of the year.

And Tomorrow Is Monday

Classrooms are worlds unto themselves. Yet shoppers in grocery-store checkout lines, used-car salespersons, newspaper reporters and editors, university professors who should know better, and any number of other rank amateurs are all certain they know what's wrong with education and what should be done to fix it.

They have no idea what it's like to place thirty ten- and eleven-year-olds in a room about the size of a one-bedroom apartment—without the bathroom—and try to control their behavior so that no one gets physically or emotionally abused, in addition to teaching them the skills needed to function and survive in society, ensuring that each child learns to the best of his or her ability, and guiding them to a full, informed life. People who find it difficult to handle two or three children at home are often the first to criticize teachers who must deal with ten times that number in a less comfortable space. They should know better. Teaching is not easy.

Teachers have risen to the challenge of educating students in many interesting ways. However, the unfortunate truth is that many of us have opted to adopt programs designed by individuals who believe that learning becomes manageable by breaking it into pieces and teaching skills in lock-step fashion. In these situations, there are clear objectives, clear outcomes and standardized tests to measure students' success. Not surprisingly, students in basal programs do better on standardized tests than students from classrooms in which reading and writing are integrated. Their major learning activities have focused on mastering decontextualized and trivial bits of information by completing exercises similar to the kinds of questions found on these tests. But children don't learn language by mastering one skill, then moving on to the next. They learn it in a holistic, integrated fashion.

Teachers would be wise to treat the term "literature-based reading programs" with a degree of skepticism. E.B. White didn't write *Charlotte's Web* to teach children *how* to read. Literature is for reading, enjoying, discussing, analyzing if necessary, and appreciating. It's true however, that a benefit of having good literature in a classroom is that students may learn to read through seeing and hearing it read by others, both parents and teachers.

Tomorrow may be another Monday in your teaching career. This book has presented ideas to help improve students' reading comprehension, ease teachers' management woes and provide students with an integrated language arts and reading program. Whether you are a traditional teacher who wants to introduce some holistic learning strategies or are committed to phasing in an integrated reading and writing program, there are strategies here for you.

Paul Brakeman, the B-29 fan I mentioned earlier, was in my grade two class years ago. Fortunately for him, I had thrown away the reading workbooks and basal readers the year before. As a result, I faced many Monday mornings wondering what I was going to do to help the children learn to read and write without the help of reading workbooks. Thinking about Paul and his abiding enthusiasm for B-29s—for his twenty-first birthday, he was given a trip to the Air Power Museum in Kentucky—has convinced me again that I made the right decision. I hope the contents of this book help you face an important Monday morning.

· · · · · · · · · · · · · ·

BIBLIOGRAPHY

Wordless Picture Books

Anno, Mitsumasa. *Anno's Journey*. New York: Putnam, 1977.

A journey through the country, a village, a town and a city starts and ends at the sea. Great for nine- to twelve-year-olds.

Aruego, Jose. *Look What I Can Do*. New York: Macmillan, 1971.

Two carabaos try to outdo each other's feats.

Bang, Molly. *The Grey Lady and the Strawberry Snatcher*. New York: Macmillan, 1980.

Illustrations focus on what happens when a woman is followed home from shopping. A happy ending.

Base, Graeme. *Animalia*. New York: Harry N. Abrams, 1988.

Words in this alphabetic fantasy start with the featured letter.

Briggs, Raymond. *Father Christmas*. New York: Putnam, 1973.

Amusing story about Santa's annual journey.

Carle, Eric. *Do You Want to Be My Friend?* New York: Harper & Row, 1971.

A mouse searches for companionship.

Cristini, Ermanno. *In My Garden*. Saxonville, Massachusetts: Picture Book Studio, 1981.

Richly colored illustrations feature closeups of the insects, animals and plants that live in our gardens.

de Paola, Tomie. *Sing, Pierrot, Sing*. San Diego, California: Harcourt Brace Jovanovich, 1983.

A tale of losses and gains in love. Perfect for dramatizing.

Jenkin-Pearce, Susie. *The Enchanted Garden*. New York: Oxford University Press, 1988.

A young girl chasing her dog discovers an enchanted garden.

Keats, Ezra Jack. *Kitten for a Day*. New York: Macmillan, 1974.

A puppy wants to join some kittens for the day.

Lindblom, Steven. *Let's Give Kitty a Bath*. New York: Harper & Row, 1982.

A cat takes his owners—a brother and sister who want to give him a bath—on an amusing chase.

McCully, Emily. *Picnic*. New York: Harper & Row, 1984.

When a family of mice sets out for a picnic, one goes missing. Happy ending comforts children worried about separations.

Nygren, Tord. *The Red Thread*. New York: Farrar, Straus & Giroux, 1987.

A boy discovers magical things when he follows a red thread.

Ormerod, Jan. *Sunshine*. New York: Lothrop, Lee & Shepard, 1981.

What the sun brings into a family's life as the day begins.

Rockwell, Anne. *Albert B. Cub and Zebra*. New York: Harper & Row, 1977.

Focuses on the environmental print Albert encounters when he goes looking for his lost zebra.

Sis, Peter. *Beach Ball*. New York: Greenwillow Books, 1990.

The wind carries a beach ball along the beach.

Spier, Peter. *Peter Spier's Rain*. New York: Doubleday, 1982.

What can we do when it rains? Spier's beautiful illustrations provide all sorts of interesting answers to this question.

Turkle, Brinton. *Deep in the Forest*. New York: E.P. Dutton, 1976.

A bear enters a stranger's house in this version of Goldilocks.

Ward, Lynd. *The Silver Pony*. Boston, Massachusetts: Houghton Mifflin, 1973.

An unusual 174-page wordless picture book about a young boy who visits different cultures doing good deeds.

Ward, Nick. *The Surprise Present*. New York: Oxford University Press, 1984.

A gift transforms a boy into someone obnoxious who makes life miserable for his younger brother. A surprise ending.

Wegen, Ron. *Balloon Trip*. Boston, Massachusetts: Houghton Mifflin, 1981.

A colorful balloon voyage over New York City and area.

Wildsmith, Brian. *The Circus*. New York: Oxford University Press, 1989.

The people and animals who work in a circus.

Predictable Books

Bourgeois, Paulette. *Franklin in the Dark*. Toronto, Ontario: Kids Can Press, 1986.

A precocious turtle conquers a fear.

Brown, Margaret Wise. *Goodnight Moon*. New York: Harper & Row, 1947.

A rabbit says goodnight to everything in the bedroom before falling asleep.

Carle, Eric. *The Very Hungry Caterpillar*. New York: Putnam, 1969.

Illustrations depict the metamorphosis of a butterfly.

Christelow, Eileen. *Henry and the Red Stripes*. Boston, Massachusetts: Houghton Mifflin, 1982.

A young rabbit paints everything in sight, including himself.

Galdone, Paul. *The Three Billy Goats Gruff*. Boston, Massachusetts: Houghton Mifflin, 1973.

Large, colorful pictures make this classic easy to share.

Kellogg, Steven. *Can I Keep Him?* New York: Dial, 1971.

A lonely child with a meticulous mother brings home one animal after another.

Koide, Tan. *May We Sleep Here Tonight?* New York: Macmillan, 1984.

Lost animals take shelter from a snowstorm in Mr. Bear's house. When he comes home, there are even more worries!

Kraus, Robert. *Leo, the Late Bloomer*. New York: Simon & Schuster, 1971.

Leo, a young tiger, takes a little longer than others to learn to read, write, draw, eat neatly and speak.

Lobel, Arnold. *A Treeful of Pigs*. New York: Greenwillow Books, 1979.

An ingenious farm wife finds a way to persuade her lazy husband to help with the chores.

Mayer, Mercer. *What Do You Do with a Kangaroo?* New York: Scholastic, 1973.

Unwanted, obnoxious visitors—a demanding kangaroo, a complaining opossum, and so on plague a young girl.

Munsch, Robert. *The Boy in the Drawer*. Toronto, Ontario: Annick Press, 1986.

A young girl who must clean up after a repugnant young visitor comes up with a "loving" solution to the problem.

Preston, Edna. *The Temper Tantrum Book*. New York: Penguin, 1969.

Animals "hate" some of the typical things that bug children.

Rockwell, Anne. *Boats*. New York: E.P. Dutton, 1982.

Boats are described in terms of their power, size and where they're found.

Schenk de Regniers, Beatrice. *May I Bring a Friend?* New York: Macmillan, 1986.

A boy brings his animal friends to tea with the king and queen.

Sendak, Maurice. *Where the Wild Things Are.* New York: Harper & Row, 1963.

A young lad's imagination takes him to a faraway make-believe land where he meets wild, towering, noisy beasts.

Shulevitz, Uri. *One Monday Morning.* New York: Macmillan, 1967.

Every day, one more guest visits the apartment of a young boy while he's out.

Slobodkina, Esphyr. *Caps for Sale.* New York: Harper & Row, 1968.

A peddler selling caps loses his wares to a bunch of monkeys when he takes a nap under a tree.

Stevenson, James. *Grandpa's Great City Tour.* New York: Greenwillow Books, 1983.

A colorful trip through a city focuses on an alphabetic approach to environmental print.

Stinson, Kathy. *Those Green Things.* Willowdale, Ontario: Annick Press, 1985.

An inquisitive young girl with a terrific imagination constantly questions her mother about green things around the house.

Viorst, Judith. *Alexander and the Terrible, Horrible, No Good, Very Bad Day.* New York: Macmillan, 1976.

A small boy can't get anything to go right all day long.

Waber, Bernard. *Ira Sleeps Over.* Boston, Massachusetts: Houghton Mifflin, 1972.

A boy planning to sleep overnight at a friend's is shy about admitting that he has an embarrassing habit.

Zemach, Harve. *The Judge: An Untrue Tale.* New York: Farrar, Straus & Giroux, 1979.

Five folks are jailed for telling what they saw. Justice prevails.

Professional References

Applebee, A. N. *Child's Concept of Story: Ages 2-17.* Chicago: University of Chicago Press, 1978.

Armbruster, B.B., T.H. Anderson & J. Ostertag. "Does Text Structure/Summarization Instruction Facilitate Learning from Expository Text?" In *Reading Research Quarterly.* Vol. 22, No. 3 (1987).

Au, K. "Using the Experience-Text-Relationship with Minority Children." In *The Reading Teacher.* Vol. 32, No. 6 (1979).

Bormuth, J. "Comparable Cloze and Multiple Choice Comprehension Test Scores." In *Journal of Reading.* Vol. 10, No. 5 (1967).

Brubacher, M., R. Payne & K. Rickett. *Perspectives on Small Group Learning: Theory and Practice.* Oakville, Ontario: Rubicon, 1990.

Buswell, G.T. "An Experimental Study of the Eye-Voice Span in Reading." In *Supplementary Educational Monographs.* No. 17 (1920).

Cattell, J. M. *James McKeen Cattell: Man of Science.* Lancaster, New York: Science Press, 1947.

Davis, Z.T. & M.D. McPherson. "Story Map Instruction: A Road Map for Reading Comprehension." In *The Reading Teacher.* Vol. 43, No. 3 (1989).

DeFord, D.E. "Young Children and Their Writing." In *Theory into Practice.* Vol. 19, No. 3 (1980).

Dyson, A.H. "Oral Language: The Rooting System for Learning to Write." In *Language Arts.* Vol. 19, No. 7 (1981).

Edelsky, C., S. Hudelson, B. Altwerger, B. Flores, F. Barkin & K. Jilbert, "Semilingualism and language deficit." In *Applied Linguistics.* Vol. 4, No. 1 (1981).

Ferreiro, E. "The Interplay between Information and Assimilation in Beginning Literacy." In *Emergent Literacy: Writing and Reading.* W.H. Teale & E. Sulzby (Eds.). Norwood, New Jersey: Ablex, 1986.

Flood, J. & D. Lapp. "Conceptual Mapping Strategies for Understanding Information Texts." In *The Reading Teacher*. Vol. 41, No. 8 (1988).

Goodman, K.S. "A Linguistic Study of Cues and Miscues in Reading." In *Elementary English*. Vol. 42, No. 4 (1965).

Goodman, K.S. "Reading: A Psycholinguistic Guessing Game." In *Theoretical Models and Processes of Reading*. H. Singer & R. B. Ruddell (Eds.). Newark, Delaware: International Reading Association, 1976.

Gunderson, L. "An Epistemological Analysis of Word Recognition." In *Reading-Canada Lecture*. Vol. 4, No. 4 (1986).

Gunderson, L. ESL *Literacy Instruction: A Guidebook to Theory and Practice*. Englewood Cliffs, New Jersey: Prentice Hall Regents, 1991.

Gunderson, L. *A Whole Language Primer*. Richmond Hill, Ontario: Scholastic-TAB, 1989.

Gunderson, L. "Reading and Language Development." In *Whole Language: Practice and Theory*. V. Froese (Ed.). Toronto: Prentice Hall, 1990.

Gruneberg, M.M. "The Feeling of Knowing, Memory Blocks, and Memory Aids." In *Aspects of Memory*. M. M. Gruneberg & P. Morris (Eds.). London: Methuen, 1978.

Heimlich, J.E. & S.D. Pittleman. *Semantic Mapping: Classroom Applications*. Newark, Delaware: International Reading Association, 1986.

Hipple, M.L. "Journal Writing in Kindergarten." In *Language Arts*. Vol. 2, No. 3 (1985).

Hunt, K. *Grammatical Structures Written at Three Grade Levels*. Champaign, Illinois: National Council of Teachers of English, 1965

Loban, W. *Language Development: Kindergarten through Grade Twelve*. Urbana, Illinois: National Council of Teachers of English, 1976.

Mallow, J.F. "Teaching Students How to Read Science Can Help Them Overcome Anxieties about the Subject and Their Desire to Avoid It." In *Journal of Reading*. Vol. 34, No. 5 (1991).

Mandler, J.M. & N. Johnson. "Remembrance of Things Parsed: Story Structure and Recall." In *Cognitive Psychology*. Vol. 9, No. 1 (1977).

Murphy, S. & M.A. Smith. *Writing Portfolios: A Bridge from Teaching to Assessment*. Markham, Ontario: Pippin, 1991.

Piaget, J. "The First Year of the Life of a Child." In *The Essential Piaget*. H.E. Gruber & J.J. Voneche (Eds.). New York: Basic Books, 1977.

Robinson, F.P. *Effective Study*. New York: Harper & Row, 1961.

Sadow, M.L. "The Use of Story Grammar in the Design of Questions." In *The Reading Teacher*. Vol. 35, No. 5 (1982).

Scheffler, I. *Conditions of Knowledge: An Introduction to Epistemology and Education*. Chicago: Scott Foresman, 1965.

Shanahan, T. & M. Kamil. "The Relationship of Concurrent and Construct Validities of Cloze." In *Changing Perspectives on Research in Reading/Language Processing and Instruction*. J.A. Niles (Ed.). Rochester, New York: National Reading Conference, 1984.

Sorabji, R. *Aristotle on Memory*. London: Duckworth, 1972.

Stauffer,R. "Slave, Puppet or Teacher?" In *The Reading Teacher*. Vol. 25, No. 1 (1971).

Sulzby, E. "Writing and Reading: Signs of Oral and Written Language Organization in the Young Child." In *Emergent Literacy: Writing and Reading*. W.H. Teale & E. Sulzby (Eds.) Norwood, New Jersey: Ablex, 1986.

Tarlington, C. & P. Verriour. *Offstage: Elementary Education through Drama*. Toronto: Oxford University Press, 1983.

Taylor, W.L. 'Cloze Procedure: A New Tool for Measuring Readability." In *Journalism Quarterly*. Vol. 30 (1953).

Walker, B.J. *Diagnostic Teaching of Reading*. Columbus, Ohio: Merrill, 1988.